What's New?

Desiree A. Lawson

What's New?

ISBN: Softcover 978-1-946478-53-5

Copyright © 2017 by Desiree A. Lawson

All rights reserved. No part of this book may be reproduced or transmitted in any form or by any means, electronic or mechanical, including photocopying, recording, or by any information storage and retrieval system, without permission in writing from the publisher.

To order additional copies of this book, contact:

Parson's Porch Books
1-423-475-7308
www.parsonsporch.com

Parson's Porch Books is an imprint of **Parson's Porch & Book Publishers** in Cleveland, Tennessee, which has double focus. We focus on the needs of creative writers who need a professional publisher to get their work to market, **&** we also focus on the needs of others by sharing our profits with those who struggle in poverty to meet their basic needs of food, clothing, shelter and safety.

What's New?

Acknowledgements

*For my husband, Anthony and my daughters, Barbara, Lindsay and Tanika,
their love, honesty, humor, strength and encouragement
For my parents, Oswald and Barbara,
my examples of unyielding faith and unconditional love
For my sisters, Donna, Debra and Denise,
my cheerleaders, my grounding place and support
For my friend, Vanessa
my confidant and prayer warrior
For my pastor and mentor, Hurmon Hamilton,
the best teacher and preacher ever...
And for my congregation, Trinity United Presbyterian Church, Flint, Michigan
my joy and inspiration; they keep me authentic.*

Contents

Advent

Journey from Depression to Compassion............... 11
    From Life to Death to Life Again…
        From Hurting to Healing
    Romans 8:18-28, 34-39, 2 Corinthians 4:7-14, 17-18

Hold Fast to God's Promises............................... 22
    Genesis 38:1-30

Risking it all for God.. 29
    Joshua 2:1-24

Lent

Developing Your Rhythm 38
    Ecclesiastes 3:1

What's New? 46
    Isaiah 43:18-21

Pentecost

When Did You Move from Being........................ 52
    a Christian to a Disciple?
    John 3:1-21

What Evidence is There of the Holy 60
    Spirit at Work in Your Life?
    Acts 2:1-21

Unity

We're Growing Up!... 73
    Ephesians 4:1-16

It's OK to be Different! 80
    Luke 10:38-42

Faith Journey

Rest in God 90
    Exodus 20:8-11

Repositioning.. 98
    Joshua 3:1-17

Be Open and Willing to Try.. 106
    Mark 7:31-37

Fear of Failure or Fear of Success 114
    Psalm 37:23-24, 39-40, Psalm 56

ADVENT

Watching and waiting for the coming of Christ, we pray for the promise of a new creation, saying:
Come quickly, Lord; our hope is in you.

Journey from Depression to Compassion…From Life to Death to Life Again…From Hurting to Healing

Romans 8:18-28, 34-39, 2 Corinthians 4:7-14, 17-18

I'M GOING TO BEGIN TODAY WITH A video which expresses a reality we often find difficult to face. If you know the song, sing along. Focus carefully on the lyrics.

Video: **"Rose Garden" (Written by Joe South and sung by Lynn Anderson)** https://youtu.be/beKFjPEU_Fw

Along with the sunshine…there's gotta be a little rain sometime. Somewhere in the back of our minds, we believe that life is always supposed to be one happy day after the next; just like a beautiful rose garden. When we're younger, we think when I get out of high school I'll be 18, I'll be of age, legal and I can pretty much do what I want to do; **I'll be happy**. Or, we think after I graduate from college, I'll get a job, make my own money, get my own place and my own car; **I'll be happy**. Or, when I get married, yup, find the right one, **I will be totally happy**. Well, not exactly, but I know when we have children; life will be **perfect**. Maybe not perfect, but once we move into our new home—yup, then, I'll be **happiest of all**! With each threshold we cross, we soon realize that as we age; as we grow in this thing called life, it becomes more and more challenging, responsibilities increase, relationships become more intricate and complicated, friends come, and friends go, heart break occurs, and health conditions arise. The task of parenting is filled with ups and downs, financial worries never vanish, elder care, loss of sight, loss of hearing, loss of mobility, loss of independence, loss of life—the older we get, the more the losses seem to accumulate and the more significant they become.[1] We now fully understand Lynn Anderson when she sings "along with the sunshine, there's gotta be a little rain sometime; smile for a while and let's be jolly…come along and share the good times while we can."

For most of us who have decided to live for Christ and walk in the way of faith, somewhere in the back of our minds, we believe that life is supposed to be different, happier, without pain and suffering. The Apostle Peter says it this way, **"Friends, when life gets really difficult, don't jump to the conclusion that God isn't on the job. Instead, be glad that you are in the very thick of what Christ experienced. This is a spiritual refining process, with glory just around the corner."** (1 Peter 4:12; MSG) If Jesus, the one and only perfect human being suffered while on this earth, we who are imperfect are not exempt from it. Don't be surprised and don't consider it strange all that you're going through because; **"We are afflicted in every way, but not crushed; perplexed, but not driven to despair; persecuted, but not forsaken; struck down, but not destroyed…."** (2 Corinthians 4:8-9; NRSV) God is indeed

---

[1] *Losses in Later Life: A New Way of Walking with God*, by R. Scott Sullender, Haworth Press:1999, pg. 14.

on the job and God will use the most awful, the most painful—the thing you thought you could not live through—use that thing to refine you and move you from depression to compassion, from life to death to life again; from hurting to healing.

I'd like to share a story with you about my sister Debra's journey. Five and a half years ago on May 30, 2010, Memorial Day weekend, her only son, her first born was gunned down and left for dead in the streets of Boston. He was able to make his way to an apartment building and wedge himself in the doorway. A man came out but was unable to open the door fully because his body, Cory's body was resting against the door. While the man spoke with him, his wife called for the ambulance. As the news started to spread about Cory's death, a thick darkness fell on my family, on his friends, on our church family.

At the time of his murder, I was away in Chicago at a Multicultural Church Conference meeting with the Pastor Nominating Committee of the church I now serve in Flint, Michigan. Breath was leaving Cory's body around the same time new life was being breathed into mine. Along with the sunshine, there's gonna be a little rain sometime. My family made the decision not to tell me until I returned home later that day. Anthony picked me up from the airport and when I got into the car, he told me. I screamed all the way to the house. The world stopped, and everything changed in an instant for me and for all those I love, and it's never been the same. We became frozen that day; frozen rage, frozen anger; feeling powerless, confused, afraid; feeling as if there was no justice; hating this world. Cory's murder was unexpected, unthinkable, unbelievable and still unsolved. On a good day, I still can't believe he's gone.

It's amazing how we can remember vividly the events surrounding a trauma even though we try to block it out. The other day Anthony and I were talking about Cory—his birthday is December 12, 1982. He would have been **33**. As most of you know, my husband Anthony lost a daughter. She died of Lupus the year before Cory also on Memorial Day weekend. She was also born in 1982 and would have been 33 years old. Many of you have lost children and it's one of the most difficult losses to comprehend. It's one of those things that will never make sense to us—parents outliving their children. Somewhere in the back of our minds, we see this as out of order; children are not supposed to die before their parents. How does one ever learn to live with this reality? We can't imagine that any good could possibly come from such an unspeakable act. BUT in some far away and distant memory, we know stories of people who have turned their tragedy into a triumph, but that won't be us. We know of organizations such as Mothers Against Drunk Drivers. MADD was formed to put an end to drinking and driving because on May 3, 1980 Candy Lightner's 13-year-old daughter, Cari, was killed by a drunken hit-and-run driver in California. The driver, who had recently been arrested for another DUI hit-and-run, left her body at the scene. Candy didn't know that her ministry would be birthed as a result of the death of her child. She used her hurt to heal.

Most of us have heard of Susan G. Komen. She was diagnosed with breast cancer at the age of 33 and died of the disease at age 36 in 1980. Komen's younger sister, Nancy Goodman Brinker, who believed that Susan's outcome might have been better if patients knew more about cancer and its treatment, promised her sister that she would do everything she could to end breast cancer. To fulfill that promise, Brinker founded the Susan G. Komen Breast Cancer Foundation in Komen's memory in 1982. Today, they have over 100,000 volunteers. Nancy's most important life work came about because of the death of her sister. She used her hurt and her sister's legacy to heal. We hear about people making lemonade out of lemons—but we think that won't be us. We all know people—our private heroes. My husband is one my heroes. His first wife died suddenly. He came home and found her on the floor. Several years later, his daughter dies. He has a close relationship with death and suffering. Now he serves the Lord as a compassionate deacon with joy and hope. He gives back to those who are hurting. My mother is another hero for me. Every member of her family of origin has died; no parents, no siblings, no aunts/uncles, no cousins—a little over a year ago, her oldest and dearest friend died. She's been hit by a car. She's been in a head on collision on the highway. She's had open heart surgery and lost a baby. She should be bitter but she is one of the warmest people you will ever meet. She trusts God and prayed her entire family into the church. Now at 82 she continues to live, serve the Lord with joy and hope. She gives back to those who are hurting.

Too many of us think that we can only minister out of strength—that only when we are victorious and can impress people with our strong points are we able to bring the most glory. But Paul claimed that there are only two things we can glory in. The first is the cross of Christ (***May I never boast except in the cross of our Lord Jesus Christ, through which the world has been crucified to me, and I to the world.*** Galatians 6:14) The cross is perhaps the place of the utmost humility displayed in all human history; the place of absolute injustice and God turned that place of death and suffering into a place of grace and salvation for the entire world. The other thing which we can glory in is our infirmities or weaknesses. ***But he said to me, "My grace is sufficient for you, for my power is made perfect in weakness." Therefore, I will boast all the more gladly about my weaknesses, so that Christ's power may rest on me. That is why, for Christ's sake, I delight in weaknesses, in insults, in hardships, in persecutions, in difficulties. For when I am weak, then I am strong.*** (2 Corinthians 12:9-10) God's strength is made perfect in our weakness. As Christians, we are called to be healed helpers, moving not out of strength but out of weakness. We can become part of this deep healing process where God recycles the damages, the pains and the infirmities and then uses them for someone's good and his glory. Your life is not your own!

Jesus is often referred to as our Wounded Healer. Jesus, the Son of God, identified with us humans when he came from heaven into a dark and broken world. He knows not only our infirmities but also our feelings. He understands the pain of rejection, the anxiety of separation, the terror of loneliness and abandonment, the dark clouds of depression. He knows, He understands, He feels. He is our Wounded Healer, the one "wounded for our transgressions who bore our iniquities and our infirmities—**by his stripes, we are healed!** (Isaiah 53:5) "In Jesus Christ, God has provided for us a **recycling grace**. One which takes our infirmities, our damaged emotions, and the garbage of our lives and turns them from curses that cripple into means for growth and instruments to be used in his service."[2] ALL things work together for the good **for those who love God**.

We live in a fallen, imperfect, and suffering world. In this world there is violence, hatred, bigotry, racism, poverty, injustice, disease—what makes us think that we won't at some point be touched by it. We suffer because we live in this world, not some dream world where every day is happy, and all of our dreams are coming true exactly the way we imagined. (I BEG YOUR PARDON, I NEVER PROMISED YOU A ROSE GARDEN.) We live in this world—on the other side of the Garden of Eden experience. In this world, evil spoiled God's original blueprint. In this world, where now, instead of God's perfect will; we often have to settle for his permissive and conditional will. Paul was really saying; it's time we face reality. The world we inhabit is a suffering place hoping for new birth in which we will be new persons with new bodies and minds and everything set right. As long as we remain on this side of life, we must come to anticipate hardships because we know that the whole

---

[2] *Healing for Damaged Emotions* by David A. Seamands, David C. Cook, 2015, pg. 159.

creation is groaning. We are afflicted, perplexed, persecuted and struck down, BUT because of Jesus, we have not been crushed, we have not been forsaken and we have not been destroyed. It may feel that way as we struggle with depression, as we contemplate ending it all, as the pain seems to be getting worse instead of better.

My sister Debra knew for certain that God had forgotten about her. *How could you take my boy away from me Lord—like that!* In the first year, she struggled to get through every second of every day; it was a nightmare that she couldn't wake up from. Her doctor referred her to a group. She was hesitant, but she soon learned that all the people in the group were in a similar position. Her journey from hurting to healing began in this group. It's been three years now and She still goes every Monday night. In the meantime, her congregation's mission was aimed at assisting those who have experienced trauma. Rev. Liz Walker arranged for Debra to appear on a local television show and share her story. Now Debra works for the gas company and has for almost 30 years. She's always been a blue-collar worker. She is not a public speaker and never wanted to be a public speaker. Now she has become the face of a community outreach program called: **Our Voices, Our Stories: The Cory Johnson Trauma Education Project**.[3] She speaks to other parents who have lost their children to gun violence and shares her story in order to raise funds for the project. She is completely operating outside of her comfort zone, but

---

[3] Roxbury Presbyterian Church, Roxbury, Massachusetts, *Our Voices, Our Stories* is an outreach mission of Roxbury Presbyterian's Social Impact Center.

she is finally beginning to feel that she is giving Cory's life purpose. *(What if, what if this were the thing she was born to do?)* In acknowledgement for her bravery, she received an award for Mothers of Courage. She's been featured in the local paper and she is currently involved in filming a documentary of her story. This is what can happen when we allow God to use our pain to reveal our scars.

Here is a quote lifted from an interview with the Baystate Banner newspaper:

"The pain of losing Cory never really goes away," says Debra.

"But Our Voices, Our Stories helps with some of the pain. It helps to hear other people's stories and realize that you are not the only one going through this kind of thing."

"Pay it forward."

"There will always be a rip or a tear that never heals from losing Cory, but I feel that I'm now in a place where I can help others understand that even with that pain, things do get better."

Debra's journey has led her from an always hurting place to a place where her hurting can also be used to heal others. God is able. Nothing has ever happened to you or me that God cannot and will not use for good if we would only surrender the pain into God's hands and allow God to work through us.

It's Christmas. Christmas is about celebrating new birth (for unto to us a Child is born, unto to us a Son is given; wonderful counselor, mighty God, everlasting father, the prince of peace. At Christmas we hope for new opportunities, new vision and a new perspective. It's about hope. Life is a journey and God is with us on the journey. Debra is now able to see God in all that's happened. Do you remember I told you that after Cory was shot, he made his way to a doorway and a man was able to stay with him and talk with him? We were grateful to him because we knew that Cory did not die alone. This man had lost his son some years back. He was shot, and someone was there with him in his last moments. This man was given an opportunity to return that good will; he got to pay it forward. Even in the midst of trauma, death, pain and suffering, God's grace is at work. Sometimes we just need to focus on the big picture. What is God doing with all that's happened to me?

If you are hurting this Christmas season—look to Jesus, our hope, our peace, our joy. In him, we can turn things around and begin to walk a new walk and talk a new talk. We don't have to stay stuck; we can pick up the pieces of our lives and move from feeling depressed to offering compassion to others who are going through what we've already been through and survived! We can move from an always hurting place to a place where God can use us to help someone else because we now understand in a way that we could have never understood before. Trust God with your pain. Bring it all to him. He will heal you, deliver you and give you new life; life grounded in faith and hope in Jesus Christ our Savior. If God did it for Debra, he can do it for you too. Don't fight this battle alone; because this battle is not yours, it's the Lord's. Amen.

Hold Fast to God's Promises
Genesis 38:1-30

IN MATTHEW, CHAPTER 1, WE READ about the genealogy of Jesus. Listed are all his ancestors going back to Abraham and ending with Joseph, the earthly father of Jesus. We find listed many of the great patriarchs of the Bible; Abraham, Isaac, Jacob, as well as many great kings of the Bible including David and Solomon. Many of us know that it's quite difficult if not impossible to bring a baby into this world without a woman. Yet, in this very long line of ancestors, tucked away are listed only 5 women. They may not all be listed, but we know they all matter. We know they all count for something. We know that the world would be void and full of lack without women. We know that for each father listed, there was a woman who mothered, however the Bible has for some odd reason, lifted up only these five women. This Advent we will take a closer and intimate look at the lives, the struggles, and the journey of the five women in the Genealogy of Jesus. These five women; Tamar, Rahab, Ruth, Bathsheba and Mary are not the mothers we might expect to play an ancestral role in the birthing of the Son of God; none of them come from greatness, wealth or from a royal line; no matriarch; no queen. Not all of them were ethnically Jewish. They were fairly average women trying to exist in the times that they were born, in the male dominated societies which they lived, surviving within systems of patriarchy, sexism, inequality; in systems which deemed women as objects, slaves; systems which said a woman was worthless, useless and of no real value unless she was married and bore a male child. In a nutshell, women had it hard.

Like many of the women today, there are so many details of these Bible heroines that go unmentioned. For centuries, women have labored in a variety of ways and kept their pain and suffering on the inside and simply did what needed to be done. Some of us have found ourselves in unbelievable predicaments not knowing if we would survive and yet God loves us, and we held on to that promise.

Today, we will hear about Tamar, a woman who found herself in a desperate predicament, but she didn't give up. Instead she held on to the promises of God. Tamar was given in marriage to Judah's first son, Er. Judah is the 4th son of Jacob (also known as Israel). At this time in history Jacob and his 12 sons lived in the land of the Canaanites. The Canaanites are people who seemingly, for a lack of knowledge about God, have chosen to worship other gods. They are portrayed in the Bible as people who are lost; who live contrary to the Word of God **BUT** who are now surrounded by people of God who God has sent to live among them. I believe when God sends us to a place where people don't know God, it's our responsibility to share about God and to live that godly example. We today, are in many ways still living in the land of the Canaanites. We share our communities, our life—some of us live in homes with unbelievers and as hard as that might be, we must continue to share what we know about God and most importantly be an example for our partners, our children and our communities.

Jacob and his sons were sharing their lives with the Canaanites and Judah not only married to a Canaanite, but he also gave his son to a Canaanite woman named Tamar. The expectation is that Judah would take the lead in teaching his wife and his sons about God's law. Judah failed to be the example and he failed to carry out what's called the "brother-in-law" obligation which states *"If brothers are living together and one of them dies without a son, his widow must not marry outside the family. Her husband's brother shall take her and marry her and fulfill the duty of a brother-in-law to her. ⁶ The first son she bears shall carry on the name of the dead brother so that his name will not be blotted out from Israel."* (Deuteronomy 25:5-6; NIV) After his two older sons died because of their wickedness in the sight of the Lord, Judah assumed that it was Tamar's doing and planned to keep his youngest son from her and sent her back to her father's house. Back at her father's house, Tamar would not be allowed to have inheritance rights or be free to remarry. Sending her back home cuts her off from her husband's family and places her future welfare in jeopardy. Essentially Judah, the one who knows God, turns his back on the law, deceives Tamar rather than risk his third son.

Tamar, after learning of the death of Judah's wife, takes matters into her own hands and assumes the duty of providing an heir for Er. She will now **move beyond the law to fulfill the law** even at the risk of losing her honor and her life.

Tamar is specifically mentioned in the genealogy of Jesus along with three other women who engage in sexual activity of a questionable sort: Rahab, Ruth and Bathsheba. These women contribute in a direct way to the birth of the Messiah. This fact represents divine irony: God works in and through what appears weak and despised according to worldly standards in order to accomplish God's purposes. God will use those whom the world condemns and include them in circles of honor.

Tamar has chosen to walk in the path of God and distinguishes herself over and above Jacob's own son. In fact, she is a Canaanite! Once again, a person who stands outside of the community of promise proves to be faithful to what God intends for humanity. How many of us know people outside the community of faith, people who didn't grow up in the church, who have no knowledge of what a Call to Worship is, or what the doxology is, or when it is appropriate to stand or sit; people who have little to no knowledge of the Bible and, yet they are somehow fulfilling the purposes of God by going beyond the law to fulfill the law?[4] When Tamar wins, we all win. We win because the son of Judah and Tamar; Perez, becomes the ancestor of Jesus. And because God is faithful, Judah's unfaithfulness did not preclude God from carrying out the call on Judah's life. God stays true to his promises.

---

[4] New Interpreter's Bible, Volume 1, Genesis, Abingdon, 1994, Pg. 607.

And so; even Judah wins because of Tamar's actions and he gets his name and reputation back and appears in the genealogy of Jesus. Jesus is also referred to as the Lion of Judah. Lion of the Tribe of Judah is a metaphor for the king or Messiah expected to come from the royal tribe of Judah. When Judah's father, Jacob, was dying, he blessed each of his sons and this is what he said to Judah:

[8] 'Judah, your brothers shall praise you; your hand shall be on the neck of your enemies; your father's sons shall bow down before you. [9] Judah is a lion's whelp; from the prey, my son, you have gone up. He crouches down, he stretches out like a lion, like a lioness—who dares rouse him up? (Genesis 49:8-9; NRSV)

Judah represents the church; people who know God yet have turned away from the ways of God for selfish reasons. God expected more of Judah and expects more of his church. But God, no matter what predicament Judah found himself in, no matter how many missteps he had taken, once God has blessed his life with promise and purpose, God made good on his word. It was in the cards for Judah from the beginning and it was also in the cards for Tamar, an average Canaanite girl who held fast to what was promised and refused to let go and she was blessed; a girl who went beyond the law to fulfill the law; who deceived the deceiver. In some instances, Jesus had to do a similar thing by going beyond the law of healing on the Sabbath day in order to fulfill the law of grace and love. Jesus' Sabbath-breaking was for the well-being of the community—Jesus, the King of Kings, dying on the cross like a common criminal was him going beyond the law in order to fulfill the law.

The Lion from the tribe of Judah is the law and will have the last say. In the book of Revelation, chapter five states: *"²and I saw a mighty angel proclaiming with a loud voice, 'Who is worthy to open the scroll and break its seals?' ³And no one in heaven or on earth or under the earth was able to open the scroll or to look into it. ⁴And I began to weep bitterly because no one was found worthy to open the scroll or to look into it. ⁵Then one of the elders said to me, 'Do not weep. See, the Lion of the tribe of Judah, the Root of David, has conquered, so that he can open the scroll and its seven seals.'"* (Revelation 5:1-5; NRSV)

Jesus as Lion refers to his second coming; the Lion speaks of his majesty and his sovereignty. As Lion Jesus is judge of all humanity including Judah, Tamar and including you and me. The Lion rules and regulates on behalf of God. The Lion overcame and conquered and is victorious. We are overcomers, we are more than conquerors; we have victory in Jesus!

Jesus faced many battles; found himself in desperate predicaments; but in all these, the Lion of the tribe of Judah came forth victorious. For Tamar and for all these women named and unnamed in the genealogy of Jesus, we are victorious; even if you find yourself right now in one of those predicaments; if life is closing in; if you are enduring some horrific pain and some unexplainable suffering and are somehow keeping it on the inside; we know that Jesus overcame and conquered because he held fast to the promises of God. So hold on and don't let go of your faith in Jesus. Hold on. Hold on. Hold on. Help is on the way. Amen.

Risking it all for God

Joshua 2:1-24

AS WE CONTINUE ON OUR JOURNEY through Advent, we hear about a woman who risked her life to save her family. The second woman chosen in the genealogy of Jesus is Rahab; a woman who had a soiled reputation. Rahab is defined in the text as a prostitute; someone who engages in sexual activity for payment in return. For those of us who have studied about Rahab or studied the Gospel of Matthew, we have seen her name in the genealogy. We know of her profession. But how often do we pause and sit with this reality. This prostitute, this lady of the evening, this call girl, this woman who is probably also a Madam—this Rahab is an ancestor of the son of God. She and her kind are included in the family tree of Jesus Christ, Lord and Savior of the world. For the fundamentalist, ultra conservative, self-righteous, legalistic; for all the religious ones; the Pharisees and Sadducees—this news must come as quite a surprise. When we think of God, we often think of holy, pure, clean, without sin—righteous in every way. When we think of a prostitute, we think just the opposite. How is it that God would include this woman, a known prostitute in God's holy lineage? Jesus best answers this question with the following parable.

"'What do you think? A man had two sons; he went to the first and said, "Son, go and work in the vineyard today." ²⁹He answered, "I will not"; but later he changed his mind and went. ³⁰The father went to the second and said the same; and he answered, "I go, sir"; but he did

not go. ³¹Which of the two did the will of his father?' They said, 'The first.' Jesus said to them, 'Truly I tell you, the tax-collectors and the prostitutes are going into the kingdom of God ahead of you. ³²For John came to you in the way of righteousness and you did not believe him, but the tax-collectors and the prostitutes believed him; and even after you saw it, you did not change your minds and believe him." (Matthew 21:28-32; NRSV)

The tax collectors and the prostitutes believed. Again, we encounter people who we deem the least likely to be Christ-like, behaving in holy and righteous ways. What's interesting about this parable is that Jesus talks about tax collectors (who function essentially like gangsters) and he talks about prostitutes. He talks about them without condemnation. He states that there is not only room in the kingdom of God for them, but there is also forgiveness and redemption for the repentant heart. Many of us believe that prostitutes and people of questionable lifestyles are sinners who are lost to the Kingdom of God and we are taught to distance ourselves from them. But as Jesus teaches the religious ones in this parable; "the kingdom of God will be taken away from you and given to a people that produces the fruits of the kingdom." If the people of God don't want to listen and heed the word of God, God will use the least of these to accomplish his purposes. Jesus is looking for all those the world rejects because he knows what it feels like to be rejected. Matthew teaches that *"The stone that the builders rejected has become the cornerstone; this was the Lord's doing."* (Matthew 21:42b; NRSV) The stone (Jesus) who was dismissed, disrespected, discarded has now become the cornerstone—the foundation of our faith.

Having a prestigious title in society, or holding a special office in the church does not necessarily strip away the sinful behaviors from our life or the judgmental attitude in our hearts. Judging and condemning others based on their station in life is a sin! We must remember that every person is a treasured child of God, equally worthy of God's love, mercy and forgiveness. Have you ever wondered why people who live on the outside; on the margins of society; who are deeply troubled; who have been rejected and displaced seem to hear and believe the word of God in ways that those of us on the inside; more fortunate, more affluent—for those of us who have more; it appears as if we have developed spiritual deafness? Sunday after Sunday we hear the word of God, but have we not believed? Are we still waiting for a sign? Are we waiting for God to provide? No, God's already done that! Are we waiting on God to show us the way, the truth and the life? No, God's already done that! Are we waiting on God to send good people into our lives? No, God's already done that! Are we waiting on God to part the Red Sea? No, God's already done that! Are we waiting on God to send his son Jesus to die for the salvation of the world? No, God's already done that! God has shown up time after time. So what's the hold up? Maybe, just maybe for the insiders; for the chief priests, the elders, the leaders, the regular attenders—maybe we come because we want to be entertained, because we like to hear the stories about Jesus; maybe we have just gotten so comfortable that when we hear the word of God it goes in one ear and by the time we leave the building, it goes out the next? It hasn't taken root.

But this outsider, this prostitute heard and it melted her heart. Rahab said to the two men sent by Joshua to spy out the land; she said, **"For we have heard** how the Lord dried up the water of the Red Sea. [11]**As soon as we heard** it, our hearts failed, and there was no courage left in any of us because of you. **The Lord your God is indeed God**." (Joshua 2:10-11; NRSV) She professed her faith in God and all the while Rahab was fully aware of her lifestyle. She began to understand that her true worth was found in God's eyes. After hearing and believing, God then presented her with an opportunity to act on her faith. So now she begins to move in a new and holy direction and the awareness of her sin is before her. The awareness of her reputation is before her. Yet the God of heaven and earth has given her the time of day by sending these great and godly men that she had heard about to her door. God was not condemning her but instead he showed her another way and she followed. Her faith came because she heard about what God was willing to do for those he loved; a God who had delivered Israel from Pharaoh and slavery; a God who moved waters out of the way; a God who provided food and water for 40 years in the desert; a God who was about to make good on his promise of land, the very land where Rahab's house stood. She had heard enough, and her heart now belonged to a God that looked beyond her lifestyle; looked beyond her shortcomings and imperfections; looked beyond her bad choices and included her in God's redemption plan.

Rahab heard about God and believed. Yet she wasn't in worship Sunday after Sunday like us and probably would not have been invited by us. She didn't have access to the Holy Scriptures like us. She didn't have a pastor she could talk to about spiritual things. She lived in a land where people didn't share the good news of the gospel and where there was not a community church on every corner. Rahab was an outsider, but she heard about what God had done for Israel and it moved her to faith and action. The Bible teaches us faith comes from what is heard (or what is discerned spiritually), and what is heard comes through the word of God.

What's puzzling are those of us who have constant access to the word of God but take it for granted. We have become casual about God (bored, sleeping, showing up late, texting, thinking about football or what we did last night, wondering what's being served for coffee hour). There is no sense of urgency in our life to follow God's leading. You see we have things, money, cars; we are accepted in our circles; we have made a good reputation for ourselves; we did it and therefore we **place God on the margins** believing somehow that **we did it** without God's help. We struggle to believe and get caught up in debates about scripture. We listen and pay more attention to books, television, to people who doubt God and we allow what they think and say to guide our thoughts and actions. We have come to believe that the church is an organization for those who have arrived and that when we wear the title of Christian we are without sin; and we have forgotten that the church is a sanctuary for those who are lost, hurting, rich and poor; the sinner and saint; the lawful and unlawful; and the for the righteous and the unrighteous.

The church is the hospital for sinners. If the church is not created for tax collectors and prostitutes, then where on earth should they go for salvation and redemption? Jesus came to seek and to save the lost. John's gospel reminds us that; ***"God did not send his Son into the world to condemn the world, but to save the world through him. Whoever believes in him is not condemned…"*** (John 3:17-18a; NIV)

So why Rahab; why a prostitute? Because God loves and cares for each and everyone one of us and will go after those of us who have lost our way. I will close with this parable which helps us to understand the question; why Rahab?

Luke 15:1-7 The Parable of the Lost Sheep

"Now all the tax collectors and sinners were coming near to listen to him. ²And the Pharisees and the Scribes were grumbling and saying, "This fellow welcomes sinners and eats with them."

³So he told them this parable: ⁴"Which one of you, having a hundred sheep and losing one of them, does not leave the ninety-nine in the wilderness and go after the one that is lost until he finds it? ⁵When he has found it, he lays it on his shoulders and rejoices. ⁶And when he comes home, he calls together his friends and neighbors, saying to them, 'Rejoice with me, for I have found my sheep that was lost.' ⁷Just so, I tell you, there will be more joy in heaven over one sinner who repents than over ninety-nine righteous persons who need no repentance."

God is rejoicing because Rahab was lost and now she's found. Now God needs the Pharisees and the scribes to stop grumbling, stop judging and pay attention to the word of God. As insiders, it's time our ears perked up, it's time for our hearts to engage God's word. Amen.

LENT

May the God of peace make you holy in every way and keep your whole being – spirit, soul and body—free from every fault at the coming of our Lord Jesus Christ. Amen. (I Thessalonians 5:23)

Developing Your Rhythm

Ecclesiastes 3:1

AS THE SCRIPTURE HAS STATED TODAY, there is a time and a season for every matter.

My husband Anthony and I relocated from Massachusetts four years ago in order to come and serve this unique and faith-filled congregation. It was our time to come; it is our season to be here. One of the reasons I like Michigan is because, like Boston, we experience all 4 seasons; winter, spring, summer and fall. However, to my surprise, the first winter I spent here, felt like summer. And there have been some autumn days which have felt like winter. Truthfully, it's been a bit confusing. As time passes, we realize that we can't count on the seasons like we use to; we have no control over the weather (it's like a wild beast). The seasons are no longer consistent. We now have snow in Mississippi, ice storms in Texas, and the polar vortex—winter seems to be endless and widespread. There appears to be some overlap and confusion about when the seasons end and when they begin. Sometimes, we are not quite sure what to wear. Anthony and I went to Florida in January for a week. During the course of the week, we experienced warm days, hot days, sunshine, rain; cool days, windy and cloudy days. Do I wear a sweater, a coat or will a light jacket do? Sometimes we have to wonder; what season are we in?

Life has often been described as seasonal and usually the seasons oppose each other. Wisdom teaches us there is a season for everything. There are seasons of birth and dying, planting and plucking, killing and healing, breaking down and building up, tears and laughter, mourning and dancing, seeking and losing, keeping and throwing away, love and hate and, war and peace (Ecclesiastes 3). For many, life can sometimes be described as a roller coaster ride; sometimes up and sometimes down. With the seasons changing so rapidly and at times overlapping, do we know what season we're in? Maybe we are experiencing multiple seasons at once? I often ask myself, am I in the right place at the right time doing what I'm supposed to be doing? Am I driving in my lane or am I unknowingly cutting someone off? Is this my season for dancing or do I still have tears to cry? Have I mourned my losses successfully or am I pretending as if I am ok—masking my pain behaving like a good Christian girl? What time is it for me? What season am I in? Clearly there are times in our lives, seasons if you will, which require us to respond appropriately. It is helpful then for us to know, to be present; to live in the now and be aware of what is going on within us so that we may respond appropriately. After all, we don't want to be caught in a blizzard without a coat.

This scripture reminds me that we often try to be a certain way when in fact we are not experiencing that particular way. For example, we laugh when we really should be crying. Or we eat when we are not really hungry. We sleep when we're really not tired. We're busy when we should be resting. We talk when we should be quiet. Or we give up when we should press our way. What season are you in and what is the appropriate response?

Let me suggest today, because we see and know that life is messy; it's not cut and dry, black and white. There will be some overlap. there is going to be overlap in the seasons. In an ideal world, we would get to grieve our losses before another one occurs; have some space in between; some breathing room. We would get to fix the brakes on our car, before the garage door decides not to open. We would be on vacation having a season of fun and rest and not learn that our homes are flooded. Life is messy and inconsistent. We make plans and God laughs. So in order to respond appropriately to the current season or seasons of life we may be experiencing, we need to be in a **consistent season of God**.

If someone asks you what season you're in; your response ought to be – I'm in the season of God. Life is filled with ups and downs, joys and disappointments, successes and failures, high moments and very low moments and all may be happening in the same week—so no matter the season— there is God. God is what is constant, what we can count on whether we are down in the valley or up on the mountain. Scripture reveals God is always with us. Seasons come and seasons go, but God is our totality. God is where we live, move and have our being. God lives within us and has made our body the temple of the Holy Spirit and has promised to never leave us nor forsake us. Summer and winter, spring time and harvest, Great is Thy faithfulness.

The God we serve is an all-season God. Coping with the ups and downs of life is manageable, doable—is possible when we invite God into the everyday events of our life. We often run to God during the low times or when we find ourselves in crisis. But the Bible teaches us that we should not forget the Lord our God. Creating daily space for God, checking in with God, praying, reading your Bible, listening to spiritual music, being still, reflecting, journaling your thoughts, taking a walk, taking a nap, crying, laughing—these things will help us cope better with whatever life brings our way. Time with God can bring revival, healing and change. Solitude and silence are essential elements of Christian faith and it becomes increasingly meaningful during seasons of loss. It is an unfortunate reality that many of us are not compelled to draw closer to God until we experience loss. Prayer during seasons of loss, wilderness, exodus, desert, valley and winter experiences can be life-changing if we are willing to journey through rough terrain and consistently partner with God and with others journeying through loss.

During my second year of seminary, I experienced many difficult and trying times. My prayer life was suffering due to the overwhelming demands of full-time school, being a full-time wife and mother, maintaining a part-time job as well as responsibilities at church. I had been going through a period of depression because I came to the conclusion that my voice had been silenced at school and I was losing my ability to connect with God and with others. I was in a season of learning about God and myself, I was also a newlywed, I was a mentor—I had so many titles; I was tired. When I tried to pray, thoughts and concerns overwhelmed my senses. It was during this period of busyness; I was introduced to Howard Thurman and learned of his love of nature and the importance of being still before God. Thurman teaches **"It is very good to <u>turn aside</u> from the rush and the weariness and the anxieties by which these days beset and <u>lay siege</u> to our moments, to <u>rest</u> in the presence of God. It is good to <u>pause</u> to <u>make an end</u> of so much that bothers and harasses the spirit, to <u>assess</u> the meaning of our lives in the light of the movement of the Spirit within us."**[5] He reintroduced this concept of **"Pausing"** to me. Pausing to stop and smell the roses; pausing to laugh, to be still, to listen to your own thoughts. This notion of pausing in the middle of busyness or pausing to experience your losses, your gains, your feelings was a revelation to me. And what he was helping me to do was to develop a rhythm in my life which included stopping, pausing, breathing, and reflecting; pausing in the midst of chaos to reclaim the order that I was craving. And so, I paused and wrote about it in my journal.

Journal Entry – March 26, 2005

"The trees of the Lord are well watered" …Psalm 104:16a

"Here it is March and the trees are barren, yet they still stand with power. Looking weary, tired, scarred and battered from winter's anger, they are still strong, tall and mighty. The tree is me; I am the tree." They are longing for sunshine and their

---

[5] Howard Thurman, *The Centering Moment*, New York: Harper and Row (1969) pg. 27

green covering of protection; the rich green leaves that once provided shelter from the scars of a lived life; leaves that mask the brokenness and death of limbs. Winter feels lonely, hard and painful, but my God is my protection. God does not want me to depend on the green—it comes and it goes. My God is ever present and ever **green**. I am well-watered, able to withstand the hardships of the elements. Even in my gray days, God can see my beauty, my potential, the real me. I am firmly planted, rooted in God. In winter, I can see me—no hidden agenda. I am exposed, my flaws revealed and my newly discovered strength made apparent to me. How will I survive the winter? I am well-watered! Even in their darkest moments, the trees stand upright. They raise their arms in praise looking upward to hope—no matter what circumstance, no matter what season. Whether it is a season of growth or a season of loss, the trees of the Lord are well watered and they know it! The tree is me; I am the tree.

Now, let us Pause for a moment.

When happy, Pause.

When you experience the goodness of God, Pause.

When in doubt, Pause.

When angry, Pause.

When tired, Pause.

When stressed out, Pause.

If you haven't noticed, we live in a society where we are mostly stressed out. Stress is a leading cause of disease and death. Even with all the electronic aides, we are the most tired we have ever been. We purchase more over the counter medicine seeking temporary relief. We are hoping for relief from headaches, flues, chronic pain, insomnia, skin irritations, and digestive problems. We have high blood pressure, diabetes, sleep apnea, carpal tunnel…you name it. The average person knows someone who is taking an antidepressant or is seeing a therapist.

We are mentally **tired and anxious**, physically **exhausted** and spiritually **empty. Let me suggest to you that we get this way** largely because we refuse to pause. There is power in the pause. We need to develop a rhythm of movement and pausing; of starting and stopping. We need more sleep, exercise and quiet time. Being overly busy is a sign of ego, pride, and self-sufficiency. It is the road that leads to burnout, anger and road rage.[6] The spirit of the Lord has driven us out into the wilderness. It's time for us to respond appropriately to the season we are in. Let us pause once again and pray: **Dear God; so many things crowd in upon us as we seek to offer you our days. Help us to pause long enough so that you might bless, heal, redeem and sanctify. We desire to feel your presence and have our minds renewed by your mind. Do not leave us alone in our desiring, Almighty God. We offer to you, our lives because we cannot live without your grace and mercy. Amen.**

---

[6] *Rest in the Storm: Self Care Strategies for Clergy and Other Caregivers*, by Kirk Byron Jones, Judson:2001, pg. 27.

What's New?

Isaiah 43:18-21

I OFTEN WONDERED HOW JESUS could remain out in the wilderness for 40 days without food. He was constantly tempted by evil while his empty stomach growled. He must have been weak, annoyed, short-tempered, his mouth dry, his lips chapped. At times, he must have wanted to die. But the prophet Isaiah reminds us that Jesus was not alone in the desert with Satan. Wild animals were present and most importantly God was present with Jesus in the wilderness. Isaiah reveals that God is doing a new thing and we can discover that new thing while in the wilderness. Isaiah prophesies; **"God is <u>making a way</u> in the wilderness."** (Isaiah 48:19b; NRSV) The wilderness experience that we have been dreading is now becoming a place of refreshment. The dry desert has become a place of living water. We have befriended the wild beasts we once feared. And now the wilderness has become a place of rest, renewal, revelation and restoration. God is indeed doing a new thing, can you not perceive it?

One benefit the wilderness offers is the freedom to be **vulnerable**. It's time for us to open up and trust God and others with our true selves, with our true feelings and emotions. You see when it's just you and God day after day; when you begin to experience the presence of God; when you go deeper with God and take in his love, you begin to open up like a flower. You begin to share with your God who knows you as you are and loves you warts and all! One of the benefits of being in a small group is that you can also begin to share and build trust in those circles. We must remember that our experiences, our pain, our losses, our grief, our disasters, our missteps, our breakdowns; our sins, our successes and our failures, our entire lives; are not our own—our lives are a gift from God to be shared, to be given; to be offered as a living sacrifice. There is someone who desperately needs to hear our story; someone who needs a life raft because they are drowning in fear, guilt, shame and disappointment. We only need to muster up the courage to be vulnerable. Vulnerability is a great human strength!

To be vulnerable means that you are **capable or susceptible of being emotionally or physically wounded or <u>hurt</u>**; or you **open yourself** up to moral <u>judgment</u>. So yes, it's scary and uncomfortable. But on the other hand, without vulnerability, you can become like a stone; hard, impenetrable, locked up, unapproachable, rarely showing emotion, distant, always business-like, uptight, closed-off and mean. We must remember that when we fear being open and vulnerable, we also run the risk of losing out on deep love; we lose the ability to laugh at ourselves; we lose out on true intimacy. We close off the most valuable and wonderful parts of ourselves until we become unrecognizable to ourselves. And then one wilderness morning, we wake up and ask ourselves; who am I? Where did I go? This is why the wilderness is such a valuable place not to be overlooked. It is the place where you can reconnect with ourselves, befriend, love, and appreciate.

The author of the book we are reading in our small group study states ***"Our culture teaches us that vulnerability makes it easy for others to take advantage of us."*** (A Clearing Space: Reflections for Lent, Sarah Parsons, Upper Room: Nashville (2005), pg. 63) If we allow ourselves to become vulnerable and let our guards down, share something personal, something painful, something embarrassing or something we consider shameful, and then it gets repeated without permission, or it gets distorted—a trust is broken, and, as a result, we close up again. We blame vulnerability; we blame people. Moving forward, we now avoid vulnerability and our belief is if we refrain from opening up, we can avoid the pain, rejection and further shame which are attached to vulnerability. But, we learned last week, that there is a time and a season for every matter under heaven—life has a rhythm to it. Therefore, if we have a season of pain, we can expect a season of joy. And we have seasons of rejection, we can expect a season acceptance; joy and pain, sunshine and rain! If we are going through life avoiding discomfort at all cost, then something within us in not authentic. If we refuse to share about those places where we feel weak or where we have been taken advantaged of or where we have done some evil, some wrong, something we feel ashamed about; it means we don't want to be perceived as weak. If we refuse to open up, then we are not trusting ourselves and others and we are not trusting the process which God has set before us. And these things keep us in bondage. These "things" keep us locked up, uptight and afraid.

We also feel as if it is our business. People don't need to know about my past mistakes. I don't feel the need to divulge personal things about my life. The message of our culture suggests that being vulnerable is a sign of weakness. This is played out in our media. When we think about the great heroes, Superman, Ironman, Wonder Woman; or people like Tarzan, John Wayne, Clint Eastwood; even Disney Movies like the Lion King—all of these heroes and heroines triumph by force, using violence, physical strength and weapons of death and destruction. These images have come to represent strength for us.[7] You ever watch a movie or a television show and the bad guy is doing all sorts of wrong and after a while you find yourself looking forward to him dying. That happens to me a lot. I'll be watching a western and I'll be shouting; kill him, kill him! And then after he's dead – I'll say; GOOD! All those video games—elevate and glorify death and destruction and call it strength. Winning, being first, being the best, getting the trophy—these things symbolize strength and if our personal stories don't end in a winning way, we are hesitant to share. I believe it takes a deeper strength to lose gracefully. Anybody can win well, but to lose gracefully requires emotional strength. Our personal stories carry with them our hidden strength.

Well, I didn't come in first place, I came in last place. I didn't score high on my SAT's. I didn't get into the college I wanted to. I've worked as a janitor. I didn't make the football team. I am adopted. I am divorced. I was never married. My wife left me. I spent time in jail. My kid is on drugs. My father abandoned us. I have a problem with prescription meds. I am bi-polar. I suffer with depression. I'm not the easiest person to live with. I'm angry a lot. I was in an abusive relationship. My sister

---

[7] *A Clearing Space: Reflections for Lent* by Sarah Parsons, Upper Room:2005, pg. 63

practices witch craft. I'm a hoarder. I tried to kill myself once. I lost a child and I've never gotten over it. I'm in debt. I'm a perfectionist. These are vulnerable statements. They reveal and inner weakness which God can redeem and turn into an inner strength. These are not stories which strike up joy, but they do ring true for the average person. These areas where we feel vulnerable and weak are the places where our God is strong.

When we consider the story of Jesus, do we see strength or weakness? Our culture suggests that Jesus was vulnerable and weak because he did not use physical strength to win our salvation. Unlike our modern-day heroes, he didn't strike his enemies down and kill them; he didn't destroy the city of Jerusalem. He had super hero powers; he is God and he could have destroyed and devastated all those who came against him; but he chose a different way. He humbled himself even to the point of death on a cross. The question for the on-lookers is if Jesus is indeed the Son of God; if Jesus is the Messiah, then why would he allow them to crucify him? After all, crucifixion was for criminals! The answer is this; he did it because he loved us and because he loved us, he was willing to be vulnerable and he opened his-self up to rejection and humiliation. We learn from Jesus that vulnerability and love go together. To achieve deeper love and true intimacy, we must be willing to reveal ourselves. INTIMACY = INTO ME YOU SEE![8] Being vulnerable means you are allowing someone to get a look at your inner self. The deeper parts of you are good; just let it out. The deeper parts of you is where

---

[8] Huffington Post, *Intimacy: Into Me I See– Into Me You See*, by Ed and Deb Shapiro, Mindfulness Mediation teachers, November 17, 2011.

your soul; where the spirit of the Lord resides; the parts of us that were created in the image and likeness of God—so let it out!

The more we practice sharing, the more we realize that it won't kill us. Sharing the closed-off details about your life, those places which have been guarded actually puts those things to death and they no longer have power over you. Being vulnerable becomes a clearing space for fears to die and for new life to begin; a place of bonding, openness, a place of faith instead of fear. Because the truth is none of us have it all together. We all have unsatisfied needs. Admitting that we need help and that we have the power within us to reach out and receive it requires a great deal of strength.

Today, I am going to ask you to do a new thing and be vulnerable. Because accepting our vulnerability is another way in which our heart breaks for God. We break away the mask of false self-sufficiency and admit that we depend upon one another; that we depend upon God; that we are limited and human—weak by nature and strong by our ability to connect with others and ask for what we need. I'm going to ask you to come forward, hold on to each other's hands and we are going to pray and be vulnerable together because when we are weak, God is strong. Amen.

When did you move from being a Christian to a disciple?

John 3:1-21 (The Message)

ARE WE, THE BODY OF CHRIST, in darkness? In the book of Revelation, John is preparing the 7 churches for the return of Jesus. And, he names some of the struggles in the church. In the Ephesus church it is noted that they have abandoned their first love; **(the church has become an organization unto itself where money, social status and power are now in first position).** In the church of Pergamum they are holding on to the teachings of other gods; **(the church is practicing idolatry no longer looking to the Bible for guidance and inspiration but placing other teachings in place of the scriptures).** In the church in Thyatira the practice of adultery is prevalent; **(the church has become unfaithful in their practices, in adhering to the laws of the land and in their relationships of trust).** Finally, the church in Laodicea has been given the title of lukewarm—neither hot nor cold; **(the church is dying and some of us, by our lack of movement, has said ok to that with our refusal to change and grow; we are not passionate about worship, about mission, about volunteering—no real desire to serve God and no real desire not to serve God; no real desire).** It appears that in the absence of Jesus, the Body of Christ is looking elsewhere for comfort and fulfillment; the church is dying. Let me suggest that the reason the church is struggling in so many areas is because we the Body of Christ have not awaken spiritually to God's indwelling presence in our lives. We, the church, are sleeping on God!

What can we do while we wait for the second coming of Jesus? How are we to cope with this void, this sense of incompleteness in our lives? One of the reasons it may feel like a void or feel like something is missing in our lives is because we have not fully embraced the gift of the Holy Spirit of God. We have denied our spirituality or watered it down. Remember, Jesus said that I am going, and when I go, I will send you a counselor, an advocate, the Spirit of Truth to dwell within you.

Before he left, Jesus finished his assignment and won victory over sin and death. "***Jesus has <u>freed</u> us from our sins by his blood***." (Revelation 1:5) We re-deemed, or we regained possession of our senses, we recognized the wrongness of our ways. Jesus came and in his dying and raising, he retrieved us, recovered us and reclaimed us as children of God. The prefix (re) means again.

What does it mean to be born-again or born from above or born anew? It means the awareness of the Holy Spirit of God living within us becomes the main thing in our lives. Jesus addresses this question posed by Nicodemus. Once again, here is this conversation: "***Now there was a Pharisee, a man named Nicodemus who was a member of the Jewish ruling council. ² He came to Jesus at night and said, "Rabbi, we know that you are a teacher who has come from God. For no one could perform the signs you***

are doing if God were not with him." ³ *Jesus replied, "Very truly I tell you, no one can see the kingdom of God unless they are born again.* ⁴ *"How can someone be born when they are old?" Nicodemus asked. "Surely they cannot enter a second time into their mother's womb to be born!"* ⁵ *Jesus answered, "Very truly I tell you, no one can enter the kingdom of God unless they are born of water and the Spirit.* ⁶ *Flesh gives birth to flesh, but the Spirit gives birth to spirit.*

When we speak the phrase born again, it evokes both positive and negative emotions throughout Christendom. If you claim to be born again, many in society associate the term with conservative Christianity, extremist; people who have no tolerance for anything different, maybe even closed-minded and rigid; maybe even someone like Nicodemus, a Pharisee. A Pharisee is a deeply religious person who lives according to the letter of the law. They have been known to come down harshly on those who fall short of the law and can be blinded about their judgment of others. As a result of their blindness, they consequently break the law they work so hard to uphold.

When I speak about being born again, it's not a magical experience where someone waves a wand, and you are now perfected and able to live by the letter of the law. In my experience, I have met many who say to me; I'm born again. As a matter of fact, a good friend of mine became a born-again Christian and she did fall into that stereotype and became overly self-righteous. All of sudden she knew what was best for everybody. She's since left that experience and now describes it as nothing like freedom.

I define being born again as an **awakening to your spiritual reality; no longer denying the God in you; and an awareness of your dependence on God.** It is acknowledging God as creator, redeemer and sustainer; it is a continuous stream of transformative experiences in your life and you attributing your existence, your setbacks and your successes; your everything-ness to God.

There are many of us who know church but don't know God. (And when I say we know church, I'm talking about the kind of church that John warns about in Revelation; the social club, the biblically illiterate, inwardly focused, lukewarm Christian who lacks passion). Depending on what tradition you come from, you might say…I'm saved or I have confessed Christ or given my life to Jesus or affirmed my faith in him—whatever language you prefer. In the PCUSA we say, profess our faith or **reaffirm our faith**. The point is you are identifying yourself as a Christian, and as a spiritual being.

However, some of us, if we are honest have not acknowledged that spiritual part of us. Like Nicodemus, we don't care much for spiritual language. Remember his response to Jesus…*"How can anyone be born who has already been born and grown up? You can't re-enter your mother's womb and be born again. What are you saying with this 'born-from-above' talk?"* (John 3:4; Message) What are you talking about Jesus?

Because we have not been awakened fully to the spirit within; we believe there is a God around somewhere out there, but we are not pursuing a relationship with God—because intellectually, it just doesn't make any sense; that's just too much spirituality. Therefore, we still make all of our decisions and choices as if we are running things; as if we are in control of daily events. We still give ourselves credit for all of our accomplishments and disregard the movement of the Spirit.

I speak to many people who leave church as young adults and then come back later in life when they wake up and acknowledge their spiritual side. They want to come back to church and REAFFIRM THEIR FAITH. They admit that something is missing; they feel lost, confused, alone, sick and tired of being sick and tired; they all of sudden have a desire or a wanting to know more about God. This wakeup is often brought about by a crisis, some painful reality or an acknowledgement of being lost and confused and in need of guidance. Being born again is the conscious awareness that the Spirit of God is leading you and you now have the wisdom to follow. Often, when we pray, we say, "God be with us." Be with us this day, or be with us in our meeting, etc. But, our prayer should really be, "God help us to be aware of your presence." God is here before we ever show up!

- **I can honestly say that my profession of faith and my awareness of the Holy Spirit did not occur at the same time.**

- **I can honestly say that my need to be part of the body of Christ and my need for Jesus did not occur at the same time.**

- **I can honestly say that my understanding of God the Father and God the Son and God the Spirit did not register until after years of practicing my faith and to this day, I am still seeking a deeper understanding and experience of the Triune God. Acknowledgement of myself as a spiritual being, submitted to the will of God, following the way of Jesus and being guided by the Holy Spirt happened over time and is still happening.**

So if we don't spiritually engage (connect, participate, mesh), we can end up like the 7 seven churches John warned us about in Revelation; and remain in idolatry, adultery/unfaithfulness, and stay comfortable and lukewarm. If the church is dying because it has fallen into sinful patterns, then the church itself needs a born-again experience; a spiritual awakening.

The Sacraments of Baptism and the Lord's Supper were established for us to remember that Christ has died, Christ has risen, and Christ will come again; for us to remember that through the grace and mercy of God, we have been washed clean and set free; and for us to remember that we are now spiritually reborn and re-shaped for service. The potter has and is molding us into new creations. We who were once separated are to be bounded together and united in Christ Jesus. We who were once immature are now maturing into the fullness of Christ. We who were once unfaithful are now being made faithful as Christ's body representing Christ and doing God's work in the world. In Christ, we are not who we use to be but are now on our way to becoming who God has called us to be. Amen.

PENTECOST

Triune God, introduce us to your Spirit. As we see and hear the wind blow, remind us that you are the wind. As we breathe in and out, remind us that you are breath. As we are prompted to go, to remain, to run our race, to listen and to be still, remind us that you are the indwelling Spirit of Truth and you alone enable us to live, move and exist. Come and hover, Ruach, in and through and all around. Amen.

What Evidence is There of the Holy Spirit at Work in Your Life?

Acts 2:1-21

LAST WEEK, WE ENDED WITH the disciples in the upper room praying and waiting for the promised Holy Spirit. Rather than taking matters into their own hands; they waited. The next move is up to God. It is up to the risen Christ to make good on his promise to bestow the Spirit and restore the kingdom to Israel.[9] This group realizes that only God can give the church what it most desperately needs. The church without the Spirit is simply a group of people meeting to accomplish their stuff. A church which lacks reliance on the Spirit but claims, nonetheless, to be a church, can eventually become a place which breeds corruption.

If we recall, Jesus' response to a corrupt temple was to shut it down. When we think of a building being shut down, our first thought is it went out of business. Someone didn't pay the bills. Someone ran off with all the money. Some level of corruption has taken place. The corruption in the temple had everything to do with financial gain for the establishment and little to do with providing spiritual guidance and serving the people of God. When Jesus shows up to the spirit-less temple, he displays a type of anger that we wouldn't necessarily associate with the Son of God. As Campus

---

[9] *Acts, Interpretation: A Bible Commentary for Teaching and Preaching* by William H. Willimon, John Knox:1988.

Minister, Brandi Miller has stated so brilliantly, Jesus shut it down by tumbling tables filled with goods to be sold for economic gain. This demonstration by Jesus displayed his level of shock and discomfort at what was taking place in the temple. He forcefully condemned the establishment and their practices. "And, when they could not silence him, they pay a man to bring him in, condemn him under false testimony, and send him to his death."[10] Corruption happens when the people of God ignore the Spirit of God in their midst.

The resurrection of Jesus means we now have direct access to God. And, it also means we cannot ignore the systems and powers in place which continue to oppress lives. So the passion of Christ is:

- Jesus sees the marginalized people being destroyed by a system

- Jesus sees the bigger picture and organizes people to be part of the resistance

- Jesus disrupts and shuts down economic and religious centers and leaders

- Jesus gets targeted by people in power and tried in secret

---

[10] Blog: http://stirringholymischief.com by Brandi Miller, post entitled "Jesus Shut It Down and They Murdered Him."

- Jesus is framed as a criminal, killed by the system so that the establishment would stay the same.[11]

Does any of this sound familiar? When you are the powerful, wealthy and connected, the ones who decide for everybody, the ones who own things and people; it's possible to take on the false perception that you indeed own God (meaning that you own the interpretation of the Bible and other religious texts and you own church doctrine).

Does anyone own God (or the interpretation of God's word)? Because sometimes I get the impression that there are segments of the population that believe they have cornered the market on what God has said and is currently saying. Conservatives, liberals, evangelicals, Republicans Democrats, extremists, Jews, Muslims, Christians -- all believe their truth about God is the truth about God; that this is what God wants and this is how we ought to do it. That this mass of land is ours and just for us and we will fight to the death for it. That this religious doctrine is being interpreted and enforced in a righteous manner that women will not be allowed to speak in church; that the Pope, the Bishop, the Imam know the full truth; that God's spirit abides in this temple, in this box—because if we can box God in the temple, then we can still have full control of all the other areas of human life. The problem is we have teachings in the Bible that contradict our way of life. Should we throw away the parts we don't like? What should we do, with this revelation from the prophet Joel: "In these last days it will be, God

---

[11] Blog: http://stirringholymischief.com by Brandi Miller, post entitled "Jesus Shut It Down and They Murdered Him."

declares, that I will pour out my Spirit on ALL flesh and all will prophesy." (Acts 2:17) Won't that be confusing and disruptive if everyone gets to weigh in; if everyone is speaking a different language and coming from different cultural experiences? Did the coming of Holy Spirit bring confusion?

Truthfully, in my short life, it has been confusing for me and disruptive for me when one dominant group gets to call all the shots and determine what's best for me. It has been painful for me as a thinking human being why my voice is ignored and silenced. It has been confusing for me why my skin color and my gender have been judged to be at the bottom of the human species. Now, that's confusing! So I am suggesting today that we take another look at the Pentecost Paradigm because what appears to be babbling and disorder is the work of the Holy Spirit putting things in decent order; the God-language of Pentecost is a both/and language, a unifying language; the language of one God in three persons. Bible scholar and preacher, William Willimon says ***"It is doubtful that Luke is describing ecstatic speech here as Paul did in 1 Corinthians 14, because that sort of speech (speaking in tongues) needed translation for anyone to understand."*** [12] And clearly those present understood what was being said and heard it in their own language. Foreign languages are not a barrier for the Holy Spirit and it shouldn't be for us.

For a first century Jew, Pentecost was the fiftieth day after Passover and it also awakened echoes of the great story of

---

[12] *Interpretation: A Bible Commentary for Teaching and Preaching, Acts*, William H. Willimon, pg. 32: John Knox Press, 1988

the exodus from Egypt, when God rescued his people from slavery. God does not want one segment of the population to have ownership over another. God does not want any of God's people oppressed.

For the modern day Christian, Pentecost is the fiftieth day after the Resurrection of Jesus Christ from the dead. Easter should awaken for us that Jesus suffered and died for the forgiveness of our sins. God does not want any one of his children to be enslaved by the bondage of sin; not the Jew or the Gentile. Passover is about the Jew; Pentecost is about everyone. God's spirit will be poured out on all flesh; not just one group, not just the leaders, not just the privileged; not just the educated; on all flesh. Pentecost is about bringing diverse voices to the table; it's about collaboration, respect and recognition of each other's humanity. It's not about ownership.

In Pentecost, the good news gets translated into a multicultural context. Right there at the birth of the church, way before doctrine and denomination, the church is multicultural, multiethnic, multigenerational and multilingual; right there in the first instance when the gospel is preached. What happened? This is a difficult truth to embrace if you believe your own truth about God; if you believe that the nations should be separate (splitting up people and families). Last week, we heard about the Ascension of Jesus. Before he was taken up, his disciples asked him; **"Lord, are you at this time going to restore the kingdom to Israel?"** (Acts 1:6) Somewhere in the back of their minds; they still believed that Jesus came only for them. No wonder they didn't understand why he spent time with lepers, Samaritans, the Roman centurions, tax collectors and sinners; why he was touching unclean folks, talking with women, hanging out on the margins with the poor. No wonder they were confused and often referred to as bumbling disciples--why is Jesus so focused on the other; didn't he come to restore Israel?

Jesus came to seek and save the lost (lost people have no particular ethnicity or culture). Jesus came to bring light into the darkness of sin, corruption, oppression, segregation, hatred, racism, sexism, poverty and unjust systems—Jesus is like a giant flashlight; shining the light on all the issues of this world and we refuse to see it. We would prefer to remain in the darkness if it meant holding on to power. If it means that we might have to get less in order to make things equal; we will shut the door on the scriptures which reveal the inclusive nature of God. We don't want to hear when Jesus says, "The last shall be first." We don't want to hear when Jesus says, "And I, when I am lifted up I will draw all men unto me." We don't want to hear that God will gather up all the scattered nations into one place. The disciples weren't interested in the Kingdom of God; they were interested in the kingdom of Israel. They didn't get that the message of Jesus was meant to be spread outside of their community. They wanted to know: when will you restore Israel back to being #1, being the best, the smartest, the ones others look up to, the ones with special privileges, the ones who are in and not out; the ones who truly belong because of our ethnic heritage, who are pure and without blemish; when will you restore our land back to us; give us political and economic power and religious authority? After everything that's happened; all that they witnessed; all that Jesus did on the cross; and even after visible proof of his resurrection; the first question on their hearts is what about us Jesus? What are you going to do for us; your chosen; the righteous ones? But of course, Jesus is not distracted by our selfishness and he says to them...don't worry about those details. But, ***"But you will receive power when the Holy Spirit comes on you; and you will be my witnesses in Jerusalem, and in all Judea and Samaria, and to the ends of the earth."*** (Acts 1:8) You are to be my worldwide witnesses. (They missed that! If you miss Acts 1:8 in its entirety, then you've missed the point of Pentecost. They heard power, Jerusalem and Judea; they didn't hear to the ends of the earth...).

Out of all those things I just mentioned, more than anything, I believe the Pentecost experience is about inclusion and not exclusion. In Acts, Luke represents the church as a unified community; that though it began as a Jewish sect, will become an inclusive community transcending languages and cultures. All the things that humanity thought were **fixed forever** changed at Pentecost. The problem is we don't like change. The Holy Spirit is all about change and those things that we thought were fixed forever are changed and are changing. Sometimes, I don't think the church likes or appreciates the Holy Spirit because of the change factor. Israel thought the land of promise was to be inhabited, owned and controlled by them forever; this was a fixed arrangement. The Europeans came to North America and claimed discovery and ownership of a land already inhabited. They too believed it was theirs forever; a fixed arrangement. Many of us today are under that impression that the place where we have membership is our church and not God's. It is my building, my idea, my ministry, my song, my room. This idea of ownership *and not stewardship* is a real problem for us. We are caretakers; not owners. The earth is the Lord's and all that is in it. Whichever group owns the land, or has the most, or is the wealthiest, or is politically connected evidently believes that they also have the right to interpret God's word for everyone; call all the shots, determine what is lawful and unlawful; who is poor and who is rich; who will have and who will have not.

But, in these last days, the work of Jesus continues through the indwelling Holy Spirit; the work of deconstructing systems and cultural norms that rob people of their humanity is still at work. Is the Pentecost event reproducible?[13]

If a church has a history of wealth and resources, then they have a vested interest meaning a personal stake or involvement in maintaining and growing their assets. The expectation is financial gain and they operate like a for profit business. They become vested in the money and not in the move of the Spirit. The Spirit cannot break through to the hearts of those with:

- Pampered flesh
- Fixed traditions
- Comfortable and unconcerned congregations

---

[13] *The Interpreters Bible, Volume IX, The Acts of the Apostles*, Abingdon:1954, pg. 38.

On Pentecost we should ask ourselves these questions: What is there about our particular context which might be preventing the Spirit to perform mighty acts in and through us? What might we be doing or not doing to block the move of the Spirit? Are we so fearful of change we are willing to miss the move of the Spirit? Is multicultural church too farfetched for the average person to envision?

Those who were present at Pentecost understood it; God created one race. The harmonizing of Peter and Paul in Acts is a great example. These two men had different agendas; but the same spirit; a different evangelical focus; but the same Lord; they targeted different groups; but with the same God. God didn't say we had to be identical to serve him. The Holy Spirit is moving us into new truth causing a disturbance in the status quo.

Can the Pentecost event be duplicated? Yes, I believe it can and one of the ways is within the context of the multicultural church. Yes, we all speak English here; but translation is not always the same. Some say altar call and some say Call to Discipleship. Some say Communion, some say Eucharist. Some clap; some don't. Some get emotional; some don't. Some say Amen; some remain quiet. Some speak using biblical terminology; some speak the language of experience. Some sit; some stand; some laugh and some cry. Some lift their hands; some lift their voices. Some want anthems; some want Gospels. Some read music; some have an ear for it. Some want a meal at coffee hour; some want just a bagel. Some want more rules; some want more freedom and that's ok; there is space for difference; we want unity not uniformity. Our preferences should not be deal breakers. We cannot allow our personal preferences to be the truth for everybody. That's not unity; that's bullying!

There are many cultures, generations, traditions and interpretations represented here at Trinity United and thank God we are free enough to be ourselves. We are so blessed that none of us are the same. And this is comforting because God did not make us all the same. But God does call us into unity and unity involves suffering;

- it means you don't get your way all that time;

- it means even though you prefer an old hymn, you get through a contemporary song because **more than the music** you have love for your sisters and brothers and love is patient and love is kind and love does not insist on its own way;

- we suffer because we begin to recognize that it is impossible to replicate the church of yesteryear

- we suffer because in order to make gains, we learn to live with the losses

I imagine that when all three congregations began to talk about the possibility of merging that there were some who didn't think it could work. I imagine that there were those who could not envision the gathering of different ethnic groups coming together to unify as one. I imagine it was difficult and most days it may have felt as an impossibility. I imagine there were sleepless nights and a great deal of fear and trembling. And then the Apostle Paul reminded the church that *"...we should also boast in our sufferings, knowing that suffering produces endurance, and endurance produces character, and character produces hope, and hope does not disappoint us, because God's love has been poured into our hearts through the Holy Spirit that has been given to us."* (Romans 5:3-5; NRSV)

I imagine an inclusive Kingdom of God where there's no corruption, injustice and hatred. I imagine a church filled and led by the Holy Spirit; one that takes its mission to the ends of the earth. I imagine the Body of Christ being open to change and not fixed and unmovable in their thinking. Won't you imagine with me a world where all nations celebrate the uniqueness and differences of the other instead of being critical of them; a world where there is no first world or third world countries; a world where love permeates the atmosphere; a world that says yes to the Holy Spirit and the spirit's ability to unite us as one people in Christ Jesus. I imagine a beautiful place such as this; Trinity United Presbyterian Church. I invite to you to imagine with me. Amen.

UNITY

God in Three Persons, give us the courage to embrace difference and not to fear it. Amen.

We're Growing Up!

Ephesians 4:1-16

MY SUBJECT MATTER TODAY IS "We're Growing Up!" We've had five years of being a united congregation growing up in every way into Jesus Christ, who is the Head of the Church. I believe in many respects we have grown and matured in ways that other established congregations have not achieved. Some congregations have chosen to remain as infants and children because they have refused to embrace the plan of God; RECONCILIATION. Ephesians teaches us that the mystery of God's plan has been revealed: we are no longer Jews and Gentiles, no longer separated by ethnicity, economics and geography—we are united; one in Christ Jesus!

The problems we face as a modern day church is not one where we are in opposition with the Jews and the Torah; but one in which the Gentiles continue to struggle against each other. The Gentiles are the non-Jews—the different ethnicities, the different denominations, the different cultures, the different classes—we the Gentiles are still stuck in first century circumcision theology and have not yet moved into living out the Christian faith as the complete and unified body of Christ. Going from 3 churches to 1 requires spiritual maturity. As a young church we have taken giant steps towards moving into God's plan of reconciliation. We have grown up, BUT we still have some growing up to do.

I'm not talking about growing in numbers; I am referring to growth that comes from the development and enrichment of Christian understanding. Or in other words, knowing and living the faith, becoming doers of the word—no longer abandoning Jesus and the teachings of Gospel and creating our own church, but by becoming the church Christ called us to be. We still have some growing up to do.

We have claimed Christ, accepted Christ, we have been baptized, have gone public with our faith, serve the church in countless ways but still remain as infants, still stagnant in our growth as believers. A church that purposely remains mono-ethnic or mono-cultural in today's diverse world must at some point ask itself; are we living out the plan of God? When you read and study Paul's letter to the Ephesians it is apparent that God is an inclusive God. God is calling the church to grow up. The church does not belong to men and women to do as we please. The church is the body of Christ and Jesus is the Head. The concern I hear at least once a week is that the church is dying. Let me suggest, one of the reasons for the death of the church is because of our lack of unity.

Many congregations are still in the same spiritual place, stuck in separate unhealthy communities believing they are more right than others; still stuck in the lie that suggests that there is a superior race of people; that people of different ethnic backgrounds cannot successfully worship God as one body; the lies that say we should stick to our own kind—this is not the message of the Gospel—this is not God's plan. We are still in segregated communities of worship because we presume that people who are different will threaten the safety and stability of our church. Some congregations would rather die than include others. We hold onto the past and worship it instead of God. We refuse to forgive—we all have stories of how someone of a different culture said something or did something that caused us pain. We have memories that cut so deep that we believe we can never trust or befriend someone different. But this same Jesus that we claim as our own died for the forgiveness of our sins—all of them; past, present and future, as well as the sins of our enemies. If God has forgiven, then why can't the church?

We are one body, yet our churches reflect something different. We have one God but it is difficult for us to grasp that the same God loves diversity and variety. We have one spirit, one Lord, one faith, one baptism, --**One** is a theme with God; one God in three persons—blessed Trinity! The mystery revealed in Christ Jesus is ONE! Reconciliation is God's great plan. What this congregation has done was not easy. You merged three diverse communities into one. This took faith, patience, love as well as pain, suffering and loss. You managed to confront the lies we were all taught and believed. Lies that said we can't work through the racism and prejudice and we can't work through different worship preferences. There were and were many who believed it could not be done. To them, we say "oh yes it can be done!"

So many Christians appear to be unhappy. But, if we truly search our hearts, we might discover that our unhappiness is associated with our preoccupation with a divided past; an unwillingness to bend, shift and consider a new direction for the church by stretching up to Jesus.

We talk a good Christian talk, but the walk is questionable. Unhappiness is prevalent because we have no peace. We have no peace within because we are not truly reconciled to God and our brothers and sisters. We have only partially understood Christ's reconciling work on the cross. Until we fully grasp that we are called to be One, to come together, not remain separate; to embrace the truth of God's word and not stay in the lie of hatred; until we obey God's plan to come together as one body—we will remain as infants and live in fear and stagnation. We need to grow up and this congregation has modeled ONE-NESS. This is why we celebrate the three in one; not because we have fully arrived, but we because we are stretching towards Christ.

As the body of Christ, we are patiently waiting for Christ's return—his second coming. We are waiting for Christ to make his way to us but in the meantime, we need to make our way to Christ. For those of us who have said yes to the complete body; we are being stretched—the hostility we have within us against others will begin to dissipate. The lies we have been told will be replaced with truth of God's love and forgiveness. This cannot happen in separation. When we truly see ourselves through the eyes of others, then and only then do we really begin to see. We see our reflection, we hear our offensive language and tone, we come face to face with our prejudice, our hatred, our intolerance---we come face to face with evil but we do it with Christ who has won victory over evil.

Christ has given us the gift of unity. You see unity is not about dressing alike; unity is not about everyone agreeing about everything all the time. **Unity is the acceptance of diversity**. Unity is a gift of God's Holy Spirit. Unity is not manmade—we didn't create it. It is the Spirit that has made us brothers and sisters, joint heirs with Christ. It doesn't matter who we are, where we came from, what we look like, who gave biological birth to us; God is our Father and Jesus is our brother and the Holy Spirit which dwells in the hearts of all believers joins and knits us together through all time and space. Church, we have unity but we also have to continue to work towards unity. We must **consider** everyone who comes through these doors. We are reformed and are always being reformed—this is what it means to grow in our faith and we are growing up! Amen.

It's OK to be Different!

Luke 10:38-42

AFTER READING THIS FAMILIAR TEXT, we generally take sides. Preachers, theologians and many spiritual leaders will convince you that Mary had the right idea. Mary appears to be more contemplative and spiritual while Martha is a practical woman of action. Mary has **positioned** herself to receive from Jesus and Martha is **preoccupied** with preparing for Jesus. Although Mary is at the feet of Jesus, I believe most of us church women align more closely with Martha. We are busy, involved and serving in many capacities. We understand Martha. If it were not for Martha, we'd all go hungry, the church would lack order and most of us would not know how to dress appropriately! These 2 sisters were different; they prepared for Jesus in totally different ways. They had different personalities. They were different. I wonder, is there room in the house of God for difference?

To assist me with learning about different personality types, I read a book by Beverly LaHaye entitled, **The Spirit Controlled Woman**. She states there are 4 main personality types; 2 introverted and 2 extraverted. The two introverts are called Martha Melancholy **(sad)**, and Polly Phlegmatic **(composed)** and the extraverts are named Clara Choleric **(temperamental)** and Sarah Sanguine **(optimistic)**. With that information, here is what I learned about Martha's personality type.[14]

Martha is the type you want on your team. She is focused, efficient and gets things done. She pays attention to details, is organized, responsible, helpful and reliable. She is self-disciplined and conscientious. She is a person of her word and cares about her work. Martha is someone who prepares thoughtfully and thoroughly and rarely overlooks or forgets anything. She can be thrown off sometimes by unexpected surprises. Martha does not like surprises—she prefers to stick to the program. She is hands on; a doer. She enjoys getting things done on her own instead of relying on others—just in case they don't get it done the way she wants. Martha is a perfectionist. When Martha gets angry she shuts down and can respond negatively to the people around her. Martha can catch an attitude and become downright mean. Because Martha-types go above and beyond, at times they feel unappreciated, unnoticed; a little used. Martha can be moody, negative, critical and deeply hurt by others. She carries anger and at times is hard to get along with. Lastly, Martha is a deep reflective thinker, analytical, emotionally responsive and sensitive in nature. She is a dependable friend, faithful and loyal. Like most of us, Martha has many strengths **but** also has some growing edges.

What about Mary? Mary is what you might call a social butterfly, the life of the party. She is someone that brings positive energy into a room. Mary has a convincing

---

[14] The Spirit Controlled Woman, Beverly LaHaye, Harvest House Publishers:1995, page 29

personality and can talk you into doing things that you would never do on your own. She is outgoing, comfortable meeting new people and a good conversation starter. Mary has a sense of humor, great at breaking the ice but also is accused of talking a mile a minute. She is warm, lively, carefree, compassionate, and a great storyteller. She makes friends easy and is responsive and sympathetic. She easily engages in new plans or projects and is gifted in caring for the sick. Mary is a joy. On the other hand, Mary's life can sometimes be led by one crisis after another. This is largely due to her lack of self-discipline and her inability to plan ahead. She is in the habit of agreeing to do more than her schedule could possibly allow. Things like tardiness, not paying bills on time and overscheduling keep her feeling pressured. Mary is procrastinator—she would rather sit around and engage in conversation about work instead of engaging in the work. Mary is not lazy, but she does spend a great deal of time engaged in meaningless activity. Mary is easily distracted and may fall short on goals. Lastly, Mary is enjoyable, optimistic and easy to be with. Both women have great strengths and both have areas of growth.

There are three lessons to be learned from this personality assessment:

1. It's important to know ourselves; both strengths and weaknesses.

2. Most of us are a combination of personality types.

3. It's ok to be different.

Believe it or not, every woman in the church does not share a passion for cooking, baking, quilting, knitting, crafting and decorating—and that's ok. Every woman in the church is not on Facebook, doesn't have an I-phone and the chances are slim that you will be following them on twitter—and that's ok. Every woman in the church is not super organized, administratively gifted and always on time—and that's ok. Everyone one can't be like Martha and everyone is not like Mary—and that's ok. If we were all the same; how boring would that would be. It's ok to be different. **Psalm 139 teaches us that we are each fearfully and wonderfully made.** We are each God's workmanship. **We have each been created in the image and likeness of God.** Before we were formed in the womb of our mothers, God had ordained a plan for each of us …**because all different types of situations and all different types of people work together for the good for those who love God and are called according to his purpose. It's ok to be different because God made us all different, special and unique.**

You may have guessed that I have a lot more Martha tendencies and, so I can think of many Mary's in my life. One of my sisters is a Mary-type. She is very extraverted and fun to be around. When she enters the room, she brings joy and laughter. We get along now, but when we were growing up and sharing a room, we had many disagreements. We fought so much; we decided to place a line of tape down the middle of our room and I stayed on my side and she stayed on hers. In high school, she attended a theatre arts school and I attended a technical school focused on math and science. She was spontaneous and lively; I on the other hand needed a plan and organized every area of my life. We were different.

Now, as adult Christian women, we are closer than ever and I believe much of this has to do with Jesus. When Jesus became the central focus in both our lives, he became the better choice for us both. My sister is a true worshipper. When I am feeling low, melancholy, depressed—which Martha's have a tendency to do, I call her because I know she has been at the feet of Jesus or she has the ability to take me there with her. After she's listened to me vent; she'll ask me…have you been practicing gratitude and giving thanks to God? Or at times, she will reach out because things in her life are chaotic and I will help her organize and come up with a plan acknowledging that step one is to seek God. Seek first the kingdom of God and all things will be added. Martha's can be spiritual too!

Ladies, both Mary and Martha are speaking wisdom and they remind us that the church's number one priority is the worship of God because that leads us to a place of love, acceptance and understanding of each other's differences. Variety is the spice of life.

There are some of us who never try a new restaurant. We are creatures of habit and proud of it. We've had the same hairstyle since Jheri had a curl. We have never travelled to another part of the country. We don't have friends that are of a different culture or religion. We drive the same route to church. We drive the same make and model car. This sameness has wandered into the church. The Sunday school superintendent has been the same Sunday school superintendent for the past 40 years yet we can't figure out why no one shows up to Sunday school. The same 10 people show up to the rummage sale and we get upset because we put so much work into it. We tell people how to praise the Lord. Well, if your hands aren't raised, you must not be grateful to God. We tell people what to wear to church. This Sunday everyone wears white. This Sunday everyone wear blue. Can anybody tell me what this has to do with the worship of God? Everybody wearing the same color clothing is not what makes us a unified body. Unity is found in Christ Jesus. Dressing alike does not keep the doors of the church open, it does not draw new members, and we are not attracting the un-churched with our same-ness. That has more to do with us—it keeps us happy. Keeping everything the same and doing everything the same with the expectation that everyone should function in the same manner keeps us stuck, stale and boring. It's ok to be different.

Let's be clear—Mary has what Martha needs and Martha has what Mary needs. No one of us has it all; that's why we need experiences and relationships with people who are not exactly like us; we need the whole Body. **Mary has joy** but Martha has **to work at it**. Martha is **organized** and Mary has to work at it. The goal for us is to learn from each other; accept each other and not fight each other.

Paul reminds us, there is one Spirit, one Lord and One God, but God has created us with different gifts, different services and different kinds of working. We are not created to be the same; we are put together to complement each other, enhance each other, balance each other out, be in harmony so that God might be glorified. We have to stop trying to make others take on our personality and do things the way we would. **So then, what can we do to get along?** There are many things, but today, let me just suggest the main thing; Jesus. If we pray to Jesus and maybe stop asking him to change folks, but instead, ask him to show us the good he has placed in them, then God will soften our hearts and lead us to a place of reconciliation. Sometimes all it takes is a sincere apology. What if Martha said...

- Mary, I apologize for losing my temper and embarrassing you in front of guest. I should have spoken with you privately. The truth is Mary, I am somewhat jealous of your ability to take risks. You sat at the feet of Jesus. You have a deep connection with the Lord. I want that too. Can you help me get there? Can you forgive me?

- Mary might say; Martha, I apologize for taking advantage of you. You have taken such good care of things around the house which I have neglected. The truth is Martha; I wish I could be as organized as you. I should have insisted that you join us first and then we both could have finished the preparations together. Martha, can you help me get organized? Can you forgive me?

Both Martha and Mary are needed. But mostly, we need Jesus; the better choice. If you are able, reach over and take the hand of the person next to you and repeat after me: **starting today**, I am going to make a choice to get along with those who are different than me. **Starting today**, I am going to apologize and look for ways to appreciate instead of criticize the different gifts in others.

Let us pray: *Lord Jesus, please help us to see the good that you have placed in all people. So often, we focus on the ways in which we differ and this leads to judgment. We are thankful that you have given each of us unique qualities. Help us to embrace who we are while we appreciate those qualities in others that we do not possess. Allow us to think of ways to motivate our sisters and brothers to acts of love and good works; through Jesus Christ. Amen.*

A FAITH JOURNEY

Sovereign God, you have shown us your glory by raising Jesus from the dead. Now raise us to new life in him and empower us to serve you as you direct. May your words be in our mouths, your strength in our arms, and your love in our hearts, that we may be worthy disciples of Jesus Christ. Amen.

Rest in God

Exodus 20:8-11

God gave us Sabbath for a reason; in order that we might rest and replenish ourselves; in order that we might have an opportunity to reflect and refresh; in order that we might listen and hear are own thoughts as well as the thoughts and concerns of others in our lives…And, most importantly, in order that we may hear the voice of God. For a long time, I knew God was calling me to slow down. Like many of you here today, I have been addicted to activity hoping to discover my self-worth. I felt inwardly compelled to stay busy. I believed that if our Lord never sleeps nor slumbers, then I must be on the right track. Because I have been driven to succeed over the years, I failed to realize my busyness was a warning that I was overvaluing my abilities and not trusting in God. My busyness was causing me to grow weary. I needed to seek God. I noticed that when I am tired in my body and in my mind it usually means I have neglected God and allowed myself to forget about God's provisions. I think and believe and behave as if I am doing this thing called life all by myself. This way of being is exhausting. Sometimes I need to pamper myself, have a night out with my husband, or play a relaxing game of Mexican Train. Sometimes I need to retreat and be alone with my thoughts and consider what God is speaking to me. Sometime I need a Sabbath of fun, a Sabbath of fellowship, a Sabbath of expressing my thoughts, a Sabbath of being still, of emptying myself. God has made provision for rest and yet we live in a society of workaholics.

If stillness is such a crucial aspect of spiritual intimacy and growth, how can we allow ourselves to live with so little of it? Pastor and Author Kirk Jones addresses our need for speed. He surmises that hurry and busyness is a serious threat to a deeper spiritual life made available to us in Christ Jesus. The gift of Sabbath cannot be realized with our present fixation on activity. [15]

Today we will focus our attention on the subject of Sabbath and finding time for Sabbath in our lives. The fact that we have to find time for Sabbath indicates to me that a very prevalent reality of our lives is that we have lost Sabbath. And if we have lost Sabbath, then chances are we are neglecting to meet God and neglecting to enjoy our life. In Genesis chapter 2, God gave us Sabbath and according to the scriptures, God has not taken it back. Sabbath is ordained by God, it is a gift from God. Remember the Sabbath because it is holy and necessary. According to Christian history, most Christians refer to Sabbath as Sunday or the Lord's Day. For some followers of Christ, Sabbath is from sun down on Friday to sun down on Saturday. Some have argued that Sabbath keeping is not prescribed under the new covenant. However, as Protestants in the PCUSA, we look to the Holy Scriptures and our Constitution for guidance in such matters.

---

[15] *Addicted to Hurry: Spiritual Strategies for Slowing Down* by Kirk Byron Jones, Judson Press:2003.

In the PCUSA Constitution, the Westminster Confessions states *"God has appointed one day in seven, for a Sabbath to be kept holy unto him: which from the beginning of the world to the resurrection of Christ, was the last day of the week; and, from the resurrection of Christ, was changed into the first day of the week, which in Scripture, is called The Lord's day, and is to be continued to the end of the world as the Christian Sabbath."* (Book of Confessions: Westminster Confession, chapter 21, Section 7; 'Of Religious Worship and the Sabbath Day')

In Hebrews chapter 4 verse 7, it states: *"Therefore God again set a certain day calling it <u>today</u>, when a long time later he spoke through David, as was said before: 'today, if you hear his voice, do not harden your hearts...There remains, then a Sabbath-rest for the people of God. For anyone who enters God's rest also rests from his own work, just as God did from his. Let us therefore, make every effort to enter that rest."* (Hebrews 4:7; NRSV) Sabbath is not lost. But in Christ, we have been given grace and flexibility. Your Sabbath may not be on Sunday—mine certainly is not. There are times when people need healing on the Sabbath; or people need feeding or need to work—Jesus healed on the Sabbath because he recognized that people have no control over when they need assistance. Compassion wins out over following laws which have been misunderstood. Whatever day you have off; it might vary from week to week; or it might be broken up in to two half days. The scripture says set aside a certain day.

Sabbath is not lost. It did not go out with the Old Testament. It is not about a particular day or a particular time. God set aside a certain day calling it today. Today if you hear his voice, do not harden your hearts. Sabbath is anytime we understand that we need to stop and smell the roses; slow down and stop rushing through everything. It is the time to be a human being and not a human doing. It's time for creation to be at rest with the Creator.

After God had finished God's work, he rested from all his work and blessed the Sabbath and made it holy because on it God rested from all the work he had done. In other words rest is holy! In the Hebrew language "Shabbat" means to cease, stop, be at a standstill, stop working, take a **holiday**, disappear, put an end to, bring to a stop, sitting quietly, inaction, day of rest and to let something be lacking (on purpose).

Are we comfortable with lack? Are we comfortable sitting quietly when something needs to be done; when someone needs our assistance; when errands need running; when there is much to do on the to do list; when goals need to be accomplished; laundry, cooking, reports to write, meetings to plan, sermons to prepare, budgets to balance, families to feed, emails, voice mails, text messages, etc., etc. It seems like everyone needs something from us all the time. Are we comfortable saying no? What are we modeling for our children? Are we setting them up to be overburdened and overscheduled? Are we teaching them the value of rest?

Bill Hybels, pastor of Willow Creek church and author of ***Too Busy Not to Pray*** states: "People who are serious about something always make room for it in their schedules."[16] Sabbath does not exist without making time for Sabbath. Therefore a key ingredient in the practice of Sabbath is **TIME**; unhurried, uninterrupted TIME. The problem most of us face is not a lack of time, but prioritizing our time. What are our priorities and where does God fit into those priorities? Is God on our to-do list? Is God anywhere on your calendar? Social outings, business meetings, work, gym, vacation, family obligations, doctor's appointments, house hold responsibilities—we have a lot of things which take up a great deal of time. When we get completely overwhelmed; when we appear to be running out of time—we call on God; the same God we rarely have time for. What if we made a decision today to call on God before things get out of control? Jesus made time for God. In Mark, chapter 1 it states; ***Very early in the morning, while it was still dark, Jesus got up, left the house and went off to a solitary place, where he prayed.*** (Mark 1:35) Jesus made time for Sabbath. It was his priority.

What are your priorities for this coming week, this coming month, this coming year? God desires to be involved in our planning but when God calls all he gets is a busy signal. People who are interested in hearing from God must pay a price; the price of time. And people who are unwilling to make time for God will eventually pay a higher price. Are we

---

[16] *Too Busy Not to Pray: Slowing Down to be With God*, by Bill Hybels, Intervarsity Press:1988, pg. 49.

willing to give up something, to put something down; something that we deem important in order to enter into the Sabbath rest of God?

We cannot practice Sabbath rest on a steady diet of activity. There are so many benefits which come from Sabbath rest.

- **POWER** comes out of stillness. (Jesus stilled the storm after resting)
- **STRENGTH** comes out of solitude. (Jesus faced the cross after praying in the Garden; it takes strength to follow the will of God.)
- **PRIORITIES** come from resting in God's presence.

The apostles gathered around Jesus and reported to him all they had done and taught. Then, because so many people were coming and going that they did not even have a chance to eat, he said to them, "Come with me by yourselves to a quiet place and get some rest." So they went away by themselves in a boat to a solitary place. (Mark 6:30-32)

Eating is a priority! We need to refuel, regain our strength, access our power and be reminded of what's important.

It's not too late—Sabbath rest still remains for the people of God. Can we find Sabbath rest today? Yes we can by giving God some of our most precious commodity—our time. We can begin by shifting our priorities. Remember this is something God desires; something God has ordained as holy. Scripture reminds us:

- Psalm 46:10: Be **still**, and know that I am God.
- Psalm 62:1: My soul finds **rest** in God alone; my salvation comes from him.
- Psalm 91:1: He who dwells in the shelter of the Most High will **rest** in the shadow of the Almighty.

God has provided and demonstrated rest for us; now it's time that we return to God and rest in his presence. Amen.

Repositioning

Joshua 3:1-17

GOD IS FINALLY, AFTER 40 YEARS, moving Israel out of their position in the wilderness into the land of promise. The Israelites had bitterly, angrily, lazily positioned themselves in the desert for an excessive amount of time. Most, if not all of them, have died in the desert. Reason being—they were stubborn, stiff necked; and they were unable to release the past oppression they suffered; they grew bitter at Moses and blamed Moses and God for the lack of provisions in the desert. They became paralyzed by their state of unfulfillment; they grumbled, complained but yet they settled and remained in the dry and barren wilderness. They were depressed and dissatisfied with their station in life and most of them died in that dissatisfaction—even though the presence of God was with them. The only survivors from the original Exodus mentioned were Joshua, Moses' successor and Caleb; Joshua's companion. They inherited Moses' two-part unfinished mission—first freedom for Israel (which Moses completed) and secondly, movement or a repositioning from a desert land into a new land flowing with milk and honey.

Some of us have positioned ourselves for dissatisfaction; for failure, mediocrity, bitterness and an overall unpleasant existence because we are experiencing an unfinished mission. We have become successful at misery, negativity and our favorite response is "I can't; that's too hard, I'm too old, I'm too young, I'm too tired!" We've either been taught these responses or we have chosen to die in the wilderness on our own accord. Imagine living a life where our unspoken goal is death! Instead of positioning ourselves to live, we are essentially waiting to die. We are living down instead of living up; counting down the years instead of making the best of each new day.

I heard a woman say that most of us have a vision about where we want to be but it will require us to do at least one thing differently in order to achieve our goal. Are we willing to do one thing differently? We will never accomplish our goals if we keep things as is; if we remain in the stuck-ness of our situation. When you have goals they should move you. If you are lacking movement in your life, then you are lacking goals or a vision for your life.

The term that best describes this state of stuck-ness is status quo. This means that we are going to remain in our current situation, the existing state of our affairs because even though we are not where we want to be, we have essentially accepted that this is how things will be. We remain, but we are dissatisfied with remaining and yet we are choosing to remain. Therefore, dissatisfaction is a choice! We are choosing to stay, stay in the place that we have been occupying, staying put, and therefore staying behind. We are choosing to possess a particular role and continue in that same state. We are choosing to be the leftovers in our life while others are moving on to a more completed state. We are choosing to halt, pause, rest, and eventually stop. We are choosing to delay, freeze, linger and eventually stay behind. It's as if our lives have become and unpaid debt; we are always in the state of pending; we are living uncollected lives; our goals and dreams are past due. What we fail to realize is that Jesus has paid it all and has taken on all our debt, all our guilt, all our sins, all our shame, all our mistakes—all has been forgiven in Jesus Christ and we are free. We can reposition ourselves because God has carved out a path for us. Are we willing to do one thing differently in order to accomplish our goals?

Sometimes in order to accomplish our goals, we need someone to hold us accountable. Israel was stuck and they had lost sight of God and needed someone to hold them accountable; to remind them of their covenant with God. And now that Moses was gone, Joshua was now chosen to hold them accountable so that they would keep their end of the bargain; not only for God's sake, but for their sake; for their satisfaction; for their healing and wholeness. If they were going to have any quality of life, they would need to reposition themselves; their attitude, their outlook and, in their case, their physical location. God was about to reposition them.

And so what Israel is really doing is coming into alignment with the word of God for their lives. When we are out of alignment, we keep veering off in the wrong direction and before you know it, we end up in a ditch. But, when we align ourselves with God, we begin to see God; when we have positioned our bodies in such a way, (meaning that we will have to move a bit, get off the couch, put down the remote, unleash the iPad, and stop making excuses). To align ourselves with God, we must open the windows of our soul; open our eyes and see God in our sight, (maybe see the Joshua's in our lives, heed the wise counsel of trusted people; allow someone to hold us accountable) so we can reposition.

I believe there are reasons why we choose to stay behind. Opportunities come and opportunities go and we stay where we are because we figure the devil we know is better that the devil we don't know. We fear the unknown; we fear what's on the other side; we fear what lies ahead. Chances are when we reposition; there will be some opposition (back to school, no money; new job, need better transportation). God says to Joshua, you will encounter the Canaanites, Hittites, Hivites, Perizzites, Girgashites, Amorites, and Jebusites. You are going to come against people and circumstances; some giants who want to take you down, who want to discourage you, people who talk behind your back, people who say to themselves; who does she think she is? Or, he's not gonna make it. You will come across some "ites" of your own; "I can't do want I want to do because I don't have no money-ite; woe is me-ite, you don't know what I been through-ite, they don't like me-ite, I don't have the right skills-ite, I hate my job but I can't leave it-ite—when we begin to reposition; we will encounter opposition. You ever notice if you sit for too long and try to stand up, your body will fight you when you try to change positions.

It reminds me of this pop song I hear on the radio all the time call *Shake it Off* by Taylor Swift, studio album entitled *1989*. As a public figure that has crossed over into fame, every mistake she makes is magnified and criticized by not just a handful of people, but millions of people. And in her song, she confronts her opposition.

"*Shake it Off*"
by Taylor Swift, studio album entitled *1989*

But I keep cruising
*Can't stop, won't stop **moving***
It's like I got this music
In my mind
*Saying, **"It's gonna be alright."***
'Cause the players gonna play, play, play, play, play
And the haters gonna hate, hate, hate, hate, hate
Baby, I'm just gonna shake, shake, shake, shake, shake
I shake it off, I shake it off
Heart-breakers gonna break, break, break, break, break
And the fakers gonna fake, fake, fake, fake, fake
Baby, I'm just gonna shake, shake, shake, shake, shake
I shake it off, I shake it off

Although the opposition is great; tabloids, paparazzi, ex-boyfriends, talk shows, entertainment networks; Taylor has not stopped moving because she is shaking off her enemies. This reminds me of Mark 6:11 which states: **"And if any place will not welcome you or listen to you, leave that place and <u>shake the dust off</u> your feet as a testimony against them."** (Mark 6:11; NIV) Also, in Acts 28, a snake fastened itself to the Apostle Paul's hand and the text states, **"But Paul shook off the snake into the fire and was unharmed."** (Acts 28:5; NLT) Taylor Swift has reminded us that as followers of Christ, we can shake off the enemy and shake off any opposition which comes our way.

God says to Joshua tell the people, when you see the Ark; this means that you have to pay attention, focus and look for the sign; when you see the Ark, you are to move out from your position and follow it! God has moved the waters back so that Israel can cross over into a new land. What is God showing you today? What signs have you been overlooking?

God in Christ has repositioned us. Jesus, because of his work on the cross, has torn the curtain down and given us full access to God. We are without excuse. We are no longer to live as slaves; we are free. We can move from debt to freedom. We can move from dying to living. We can move from dissatisfaction to satisfaction; from failure to success; from bitterness to betterment. In Christ, we have been placed in a different position but now we have to choose to walk in it (materialize, to manifest, to allow the word now placed in our hearts to become flesh, to be in sync). In order to cross over we must readjust ourselves and this will upset the status quo. Are we willing to do one thing differently?

If you have been paying close attention to what's been going on in the life of this congregation over the past 12 months, you would have noticed that God has repositioned us; we have crossed over from a church dominated by debt to a church motivated by mission. Last year this time we were unable to pay our mortgage, this year we are not only making the monthly payments, but we have made extra payments. Why? Because we moved out from our positions and followed the word of God. Last fall, God gave us a choice; we had come to a defining moment. With that choice, God gave us a plan and we followed it. That plan came from this same book, Joshua, and this same chapter, chapter 3; verses 1 through 7. And the plan was as follows:

God's Plan for Managing Crisis

1. Wait for God.

2. Trust God to Lead.

3. Sanctify yourselves.

4. Take the first step of faith.

Every step of this plan required us to move out from our positions and follow God into uncertainty. And yes, we have encountered opposition, (problems with the heating and air conditioning; losing our music director; increase in capital giving and decrease in operations) but we are going to shake it off and keep moving because it's gonna be alright.

We are learning to wait on God and not just move at our own speed. We are learning to discern the voice of God. God was waiting on us to become more mission-minded; more externally concerned and not so internally focused. God wanted us to trust in his lead and, to also trust in the leadership he has provided. Israel had to trust in what Joshua was saying. Trust in the wise counsel. And then God instructs that we must sanctify ourselves (focus on our individual relationship with God; communicate with God on a regular basis; study the scriptures; love and serve one another). And finally, God says get ready to move and take that first step of faith. Maybe it's your time that God wants. It's time for you to show up on Sunday and it's time for you to allocate some of your personal time not only for Sunday worship but also to use your gifts and talents for service. God desires your gifts and talents; it's time to use those gifts and serve on a team, take part in worship, visit the sick, and be the hands and feet of Christ in your community. God says it's time for us to take the first step of faith and give of your treasure and do not offer unto God that which costs you nothing. God has and continues to reposition us. It's time to move into a place of satisfaction and fulfillment. Wherever God is leading you; move into that new place. It's gonna be alright. We are going to be alright. "I've gotta feeling everything's gonna be alright; be alright, be alright, be alright."[17] Amen.

---

[17] *I've Got a Feeling* by Florida Boys, 1995.

Be Open and Willing to Try

Mark 7:31-37

DURING THIS TIME IN JESUS' ministry, he has already called the twelve. They have been set apart to extend the work of Jesus' ministry. The term apostle, meaning sent ones, was first used in Mark. It states; "The apostles gathered around Jesus and reported to him all they had done and taught." (Mark 6:30; NIV) The apostles were being sent out. The twelve included, Simon called **Peter**, his brother **Andrew**, **John** and **James**, the sons of Zebedee, **Philip**, **Bartholomew**, **Matthew**, **Thomas**, **Simon** the Zealot, **James**, son of Alphaeus, **Judas**, son of James and **Judas** Iscariot. They were instructed by Jesus to travel light in view of the urgency of their mission and as a sign of their reliance on God alone to accomplish it. As followers of Jesus we must simplify our lives—trim back, purge, declutter and become more mobile. When we acquire too much stuff, we often make a choice to keep the stuff rather than laying it aside to follow Jesus. He instructs them to accept whatever hospitality is offered them when they enter a village and not to go shopping about for better accommodations. This will keep their minds and energies focused on the appointed task—which is to announce the Kingdom of God. The only resource the apostles took with them was the authority they had received from Jesus. Jesus also tells them how to respond when people refuse to receive or to hear their message. They are to "shake off the dust that is on their feet as a warning against them." (Mark 6:11) This gesture symbolizes separation and warns those who were unreceptive of the danger they incur in rejecting these messengers. Don't linger seeking to persuade those who refuse the message, but move on. That's not to say that the opportunity will not present itself again, but for now—move on. The disciples went out two by two. Their ministry included preaching, teaching, exorcizing demons, and healing in his name, relying on no resource except the authority of Jesus Christ.

Although the twelve walked alongside Jesus from place to place, they still did not really understand him. They were always vowing and trying to follow him, but their repeated failures speaks to their doubts about Jesus and ironically, their need for Jesus' direction. The wonderful thing about following Jesus is that Jesus does not wait for us to fully understand or for us to become flawless disciples before we can associate with him or participate in his mission. Flawed as they were, he sends them out. This is a reminder to us that we are to stop waiting, hesitating and holding back. Stop trying to reach perfection before we decide to follow Jesus.

Our text today is the last in a sequence of miracle stories concerned with the question of Jesus' identity. When Jesus was preaching in his home town of Nazareth, the hearers were amazed and wondered "What's this wisdom that has been given him that he even does miracles! *"Isn't this the carpenter? Isn't this Mary's son and the brother of James, Joseph, Judas and Simon? Aren't his sisters here with us? After this Jesus went around teaching from village to village."* (Mark 6:3, 6b; NIV) The people from his hometown were confused about whom they knew him to be and who he was becoming. Sometimes, people want you to be who they need you to be and not who you are meant to be. Sometimes people are not comfortable with your gifts. They become jealous, envious and mean-spirited towards you. In the case of his hometown, Jesus did what he told his disciples to do when they are rejected…shake the dust off and move on. And now Jesus is on the move proclaiming that the Kingdom of God has come near. The word is getting out about his ability to perform miracles and heal the sick. Jesus repeatedly commanded those he had healed not to tell what they had seen, but word began to spread throughout the Decapolis about his miraculous powers.

The text states "they" or "some people" (according to the NIV translation) brought a deaf man who could hardly talk to Jesus and they begged Jesus to place his hand on the man. Who are these people? They are unnamed and we know nothing of their background. We don't know if any of them had ever seen Jesus or if they heard him preaching in the synagogue. We don't know if any of them were friends with the leprous man or the paralytic that Jesus healed earlier. Or maybe they were on the mountainside that day when Jesus fed the 5000. Were they Jew or Gentile—the Bible doesn't say? It states they or some people brought this man to Jesus.

What we can ascertain is that somebody in that group believed that Jesus could do something to help this man. Somebody in that group had enough faith to convince the others to bring this person to Jesus. Someone had to be sick and tired of the present situation. Someone was ready for change and wanted something better. Someone was willing to risk it all. Someone else in the group had to be open enough to go along. All of them had to be willing to try.

Sometimes a situation gets to be toxic. You get to a point where something has to be done. The first thing you try may not work. Maybe this deaf man had been to doctors or to people who claimed they could heal him but instead they took his money, made promises but he was never healed. What was evident is that people who had some form of illness or handicap or physical ailment that was undiagnosed were deemed unclean. If you had some sort of external condition; something that was apparent on the outside—you were ostracized. This leads us to believe that "they" or the people who brought the man to Jesus cared about him and weren't embarrassed by his physical condition. Maybe they were family or close and trusted friends. This should be a reminder to us that as family members and friends, we are positioned to bring our loved ones to Jesus. Many of them have closed their ears and refused to hear about the healing powers of Jesus. If we are not inviting them or bringing them—we might ask ourselves are we embarrassed by them. Or are we embarrassed to share with them about our faith in Jesus? The "they" in this text are functioning as disciples of Jesus. They not only have faith in Jesus, but they are acting on it. And once they catch up with Jesus, the text states; **"they begged him."** (Mark 7:32; NIV) They had no shame because they desperately wanted healing and wholeness for this man.

If we keep ourselves opened to the Spirit of God, we will be led to invite or bring someone to church and then trust Jesus to do the rest. Sometimes, we have to do something different; something out of the ordinary in order to get different results. We must be willing to give something a try! They had never done anything like this before, yet they trusted in Jesus. They stepped outside of their cultural and religious box. They could have alienated their brother—which was what the tradition of the Jews instructed them to do. According to their interpretation of the law, Jews did not associate, befriend, or come into contact with the unclean! If they had continued to do what was always done, then the spreading of the Gospel may have stagnated and possibly this man would not have received his healing. This tells me that in order for the Gospel of Jesus Christ to continue to spread to the *"theys"* of this world, we must be willing to give something else a try! Trying something new doesn't mean it's permanently etched in stone. If it doesn't work, we try something else. But to remain spiritually deaf when healing is available seems like willful resistance; prideful arrogance and disobedience to the Spirit of God.

After "they" had successfully accomplished their mission of getting the deaf man to Jesus, the text states that Jesus **"took him aside, away from the crowd."** (Mark 7:33; NIV). I think this is important to lift up because we must remember that it is not our job to fix people. It is not our job to save people—Jesus saves! It is not our job to set people straight and point out all that's wrong with them. Jesus has a way of dealing with our imperfections, our flaws, and our sins in private. He will take us aside, away from the crowd. When the Lord reveals these things to you—things you need to work on; things you need to stop doing and things you need to start doing—when God reveals these things to you in private, my advice to you is to take heed. The Lord's ways are gentle and filled with compassion. However, if we fail to obey, I believe, the lessons become harder, more intense and eventually become public—what was meant for private becomes public. The healing lesson he gave to the deaf man was in private and the message was "be open." I believe this message had physical, emotional and spiritual meaning.

Be open to the Spirit of God. Be open to life. Be open to others. Be open to change. Be open to trying new things. Be open to where you are being led. Be open to love. Be open to friendship. Be open to service. Be open to prayer. Be open to worship. Be open to Bible Study. Be open to Sunday school. Later on this morning, you will hear about a shift we are hoping to make in Sunday school. Some of you have already heard about it. Some of you may have already made up your mind that it won't work before giving it a try. The truth is we have very poor attendance at Sunday school. The truth is very few people are committed to being here at 9:15am on Sunday morning. Yet the teachers are here prepared and ready. The truth is if we don't continue to learn and grow in the word of God, we eventually stagnate, fall away, lose our zeal and excitement for God, for worship, for church and down and down and down we go. God is revealing to us today, just as he did over 2000 years ago to the deaf mute-- be open! Be open and be willing to try anything that will advance the kingdom of God.

Now is the time to open our minds up to new possibilities. What does it mean to be open-minded? It means that even if you think you are right, you know that you can be wrong and are always willing to listen to and hear an opposing or contradictory view. You train your mind to be receptive to new ideas. On the other hand, a close-minded person is rigid in their opinions and narrow in their outlook. They are unwilling to try new things and more inclined to condemn anything untraditional. They are often viewed as intolerant, inflexible and stuck.

Just imagine if Jesus were closed minded and unwilling to try something new. As far as I know, no one had ever died so that all of humanity might be saved. No one had taken on all of the sins of the world and bled forgiveness on all of the sins of the world. It had not been done before. It was not the traditional way for sins to be atoned. Most people didn't believe it would work—they were close-minded. Even the disciples didn't want to hear about what Jesus was proposing. They closed their ears. But someone, despite the naysayers, despite the doubters, despite the resistance, was open and willing to try. Someone had enough faith in God to be willing to make the sacrifices, be ridiculed, be spat on, be beaten, and be humiliated for us. Someone was sick and tired of the human condition. Someone was ready for a change and wanted something better for us. Someone was willing to risk it all for us.

Jesus said yes to God's plan and after he was crucified, died and rose from the grave—Jesus became our plan; yours and mine. We are his disciples and its time we follow even if it's unconventional, even if we have never done it this way; even if it's risky, even if it causes us some discomfort—let's be willing, and open to give it a try. Amen.

Fear of Failure or Fear of Success

Psalm 37:23-24, 39-40, Psalm 56:13

OUR STEPS ARE MADE FIRM BY the Lord. God is getting us ready to take a step like we've never taken before. Our next steps are usually pretty predictable. We know exactly what we must do next—after 1 comes 2, after A comes B. Some of us knew our next steps after high school would be college; for some it was a job, for some a wedding and children. Some of us already know the next step today after worship—coffee hour, Sunday school, maybe meeting up with friends, going home to make dinner or to watch all day football! We know the next steps because we are creatures of habit mostly doing the orderly thing, the thing that comes before and the thing which naturally follows after. Is anyone flying to New York City today to see a play? Is anyone intentionally trying a new recipe today? We are used to our routines. We get up, use the bathroom, brush our teeth, shower, have coffee, get dressed, run errands, go to work, doctor appointments, volunteer, have dinner, watch television, talk on the phone, and go to bed. In may not be in that order, but that's pretty much the routine. My question for you today is: Do you ever get bored? Are the steps you take boring? Do you have anything interesting to share with the people in your life?

Not only are our steps made firm by the Lord—when we walk with the Lord, our steps become very interesting. God is interested in taking our boring, predictable, and comfortably dull steps and ordering them according to his plan. In order to change what you do, you must be willing to address the fear which holds you back from steering off course. I recently heard a preacher say, the first rule of change is we must be willing to break the rules! He was not suggesting anything illegal or unethical; but maybe something unorthodox. The word orthodox simply means right, established, traditional or accepted. If you are orthodox, then that means you adhere closely to the rules and desire to be proper in all you do. We have things that we do and we have a set way of doing them and if someone suggests another way, an alternative way; we get bent out of shape, stressed and worried. We say "why change what's working?" Question: Who's it working for? Maybe those steps worked for June Cleaver, but it may be a hindrance for Oprah Winfrey. Maybe those predictable steps once taken before the Civil Rights Act of 1964 are no longer permissible in 2015. Maybe what was once orthodox is now oppressive. There comes a time when we have to look carefully at the steps we have become programmed to take and recognize that we need to go another way. We need to reform, reorganize, modify, and revolutionize our steps. I'm talking about the steps which have been ordered by the Lord!

We need to admit that we are afraid of reformation. You see we believe that if we follow the old patterns, then we are certain that everything will turn out right. We don't want to be stumbling around in the dark. Why should we reinvent the wheel? Well, the first wheel invented was a potter's wheel around 3500 BC. The wheel for transportation was not invented until 300 years or so after because someone decided to take the wheel in a different direction. Thank God someone reinvented the wheel! The truth is we fear failure—yet our failure is built into God's plan. The Bible says: "though we stumble." What does it mean to stumble? STUMBLE: Faltering or falling in the course of running or walking. Stumbling is also is referred to as failure, hesitation or difficulty. As wise as we may be, as sure of our ways as we are, as much as we trust our routines more than we trust in God—the wise person is not perfect; they will fall. But God guides and protects them even when they sin and encounter obstacles.

The thing we fear most about falling or stumbling is the pain. Falling HURTS! Have you ever fallen outside on the street, in public? EMBARRASING! People are staring, pointing—you become the center of unwanted attention. Some will even laugh. Some will come and offer help. If you are carrying a purse or a bag—the items may be all over the place. It's embarrassing and your pride is HURT! Falling hurts. When you fall, chances are great that you will hurt yourself. You're sore, achy but all you care about is getting up quickly hoping that no one has seen the fall. Hopefully nothing is broken because now you will have to rely on the kindness of strangers to help you. It's hard enough asking people you know to help you—never mind strangers! If nothing's broken, then you might be bruised, you may have scraped up your skin or dirtied your clothing. Your pride is hurt. Your body is hurting. You're embarrassed, you might even feel ashamed. You feel like a loser! Falling hurts. Falling draws negative attention. It draws pity. We don't like to fall and we don't like to fail. Failing messes with our egos—especially if our failure is public and affects others. Failing can set us back.

We may have to start over. We may have to take advice from others. We may have to apologize and own our mistake. We may even decide to quit or give up. Whatever you call it: falling, failure or stumbling—we want no part of it and we will do all we can do to avoid it. Yet, it is inevitable; "though we stumble." Question: Is there anything in life that you are passionate about pursuing that you are willing to fall, fail or stumble to achieve it?

Mistakes are not to be avoided. Just read the Bible and you will see our Bible heroes and heroines making one mistake after another. The story of Abraham and Sarah are filled with human mistakes and missteps. Mistakes are signals that you're moving into new territory, breaking new ground, making progress. It's impossible to break new ground without breaking old rules. There's an old English proverb that states: "He who makes no mistakes never makes anything."

If we agree that falling is inevitable, then our focus should not be on the falling but instead, it should be on the getting back up! What we do after we've fallen can determine whether we stay stuck or whether we move forward. We're not interested in bouncing back, we are interested in bouncing forward! This means that we want to learn and grow from our failures and mistakes. Believe it or not, the more times we fall and get back up, the stronger we get, the more resilient we become. The difference between average people and achieving people is their approach to falling, failure and stumbling.

Leadership expert, John Maxwell, gives us a new understanding of failure. He teaches in his book, *Failing Forward*, that failure is unavoidable for human beings. There are no mistakes, only lessons. If we don't learn, the lessons get harder. You know you've learned when you've changed! We believe failure is the enemy – however it takes adversity to create success. We believe failure is final—it's not. "All roads to success lead us through lands of failure. Each of us has a choice to make. Are we going to keep our boring routines, sleep our life away in order to avoid failure at all costs? Or are we going to wake up and realize this: Failure is simply a price we play to achieve success."[18]

God is getting us ready to take a step of faith; one that involves risk; one that includes some experimentation and exponential thinking; one that will break the rules and break the established patterns; one that may cause us to stumble. Though we stumble, we shall not fall headlong, we shall not be utterly cast down, we are not down for long and we are not down for the count, the Lord will steady us. The Lord will hold us by the hand. We are under the Lord's arm; God has a grip on us. Why; because God expects us to fall; not backwards but forwards. Because of God's grace, the falling is not the problem. The falling has been built into the plan and is covered in the saving and forgiving grace of Jesus Christ. Psalm 56:13 states: "For you have delivered me from death and my feet from stumbling, that I may walk before God in the light of life." Amen.

---

[18] *Failing Forward: Turning Mistakes into Stepping Stones for Success* by John C. Maxwell, Thomas Nelson:2000, pages 13-18.

www.ingramcontent.com/pod-product-compliance
Lightning Source LLC
Chambersburg PA
CBHW052156110526
44591CB00012B/1972